# Always Different
## Poems of Memory

# Gyula Jenei

Translated by Diana Senechal

PHONEME
MEDIA

DEEP
VELLUM

DALLAS, TEXAS

Phoneme Media, an imprint of Deep Vellum
3000 Commerce St., Dallas, Texas 75226
deepvellum.org · @deepvellum

Deep Vellum is a 501c3 nonprofit literary arts organization
founded in 2013 with the mission to bring
the wrld into conversation through literature.

First Edition, 2022

Library of Congress Control Number: 2022931017

ISBN (TPB) 978-1-64605-123-6
ISBN (Ebook) 978-1-64605-124-3

Front cover by Justin Childress. | justinchildress.co
Layout and typesetting by KGT

PRINTED IN THE UNITED STATES OF AMERICA

# Contents

# Standing Point

forty years from now that street would be barely
familiar—i would amble down it through ultraviolet beams—
the dirt road with its furrows would by then
be asphalted over, instead of tractors and horsecarts,
cars would ride upon it; the houses plastered
throughout, roofs renovated, small checkered windows
replaced with larger ones, a few of the houses demolished,
new ones built in their place. the fences would change too,
lilacs and other shrubs would disappear or else
sprout up out of nowhere, the old trees would be cut down,
the saplings would have grown to full size, like the girls,
who by then would have become old women, and i would not
recognize them, at best the other way around, since i
would not have changed much on the surface. besides,
who could it be who, searching the past one scorching noon,
would look this way and that in front of an entrance, then,
hesitating, move on to peruse more houses or at least
track down a familiar face among the old neighbors,
but the old neighbors would have dwindled away,
would have vanished into the cemetery, into nothingness,
and their children in poverty, scattered here and there
in faraway cities. mostly new families would live on that
barely familiar street, by and large just like the
old ones, except that just about everyone would have

a tv. forty years from now there would be no one left

for me to visit. it would be a little like intruding.

my face and neck would be covered with fifty-factor

sunscreen, which after a while would feel scanty.

the sun would bake my skin, which is how it is even when

everything on that street is still familiar. but forty years

from now i would worry that my defense was imperfect,

would fear a sunburn, skin cancer. yet i would venture out

to the scantily shaded street's end, where the lower part

of the pasture begins, and where the water collects after

a rain, and in that clean translucent puddle it is good

to run around and hear my soaked shoes' smacking sound

with every step. forty years from now there would be no

trampled grass paths toward the farms, the cemetery,

nor would the hoofprints of cattle be kept intact

by the dry gray earth until the next big rain. forty

years from now i would then turn around in summer

at the road's end, and take the paved way back. glancing

around i would seek, at one crossroads, the second house.

the home of a friend's family, so much time i spent there, but

still i would not recognize the building if i did not know

that it had to be right there. forty years from now, everything

would be different: extensions built, new coats of paint,

fences changed, a garage heaved into the place where

the coops used to be, different toys scattered around the yard,

clothes hanging out to dry, and i would duck quickly

out of sight lest the person leaving the house ask me

who i am looking for. i would make my escape into the

just barely familiar street. the old sidewalk, i would mumble
to myself, and in this manner would adjust
my footsteps. stooping under a tree overhanging
the road, i would barely make it through, and as soon
as i turned the corner—as when a person snaps out
of dizziness or a dream—all of a sudden
i would not know where i was, so unfamiliar
the terrain, i would look all around frightened,
and would then feel the true dizziness coming on,
when a few meters ahead, across the street,
i would make out the house where i am to live
until the age of seventeen and where, if i look out
through the window, i see—my standing point—
exactly that same corner.

# Yard

one day i set down in writing the place where my childhood goes by:
the house, the chicken-shat yard, the garden, sunken into apathy,
i set down the mysterious shed used as a trash bin, where
my grandparents' discarded items are gathering dust, waiting
for someone to take something out from their midst. i set down
the spirit level that i find there, the rusty wrench,
the discarded bedside chest of drawers, the marble slab leaning
against an inner wall, the bedrests, the huge, round grain container
made of tin, which we fill with purchased wheat once a year, to sink
eggs into, since they last longer that way. i set down
the ratty *latertheywillservesomepurpose* clothes hanging on the line,
the blinded wall mirror, the woodpile in the yard, the flat-roofed
shed that houses the garden tools, wheelbarrow, cauldron,
cauldron stand, the other storage room, whose loft entrance, always open,
i clamber through from the coal heap, without a ladder, and above
the chicken- and pigshed, in the overhanging attic, i find baffling
quantities of newspapers and books: old magazines, an issue of *tolnai
világlapja*, cowboy stories, stories of the underworld. i push or prop up
a tile or two. the sun overheats the roof, sweat flows from me,
i fight like a legionnaire in rejtő novels, and i keep on sweating for hours
in the attic, the dust, the mouse-scented stuffiness, but i love to read there.
sometimes the cat stretches out wide behind my back. i set down
the chicken-feed spread out on the ground, the sharp iron pieces
called cornhuskers. with these we cut a line into the cob so that

it will be easier to husk the rest with our palms. i set down the fountain,

the ducks drunk on mulberries, the rings in the pigs' noses,

the clattering of the wash bucket, the dog chain, or, in the backyard,

the maize stems, bound together in sheaves, stacked on top of each other,

the stalk pile, where i can play castle with the kids next door,

or maybe alone too. i set down

the fallen summer apples, the hedgehogs scampering along

the wire fence in the evenings, the smell of elderberry, garbage heap

and raw earth, the smell of rain, of the backyard outhouse, of poverty,

and also that i learn as a kid that poor people are not just those

who do not work, since my father works hard, my mother works

hard too, my grandmother does what she can as a wrinkled

old woman, she tends the animals, cooks, sews; because, she says,

it is a shame to go around in tattered clothes, but not in stained ones.

yet i will not believe her, and will be ashamed of my stained

old wearables.

# Photographs

in the first picture of me it will be summer: a few months old,

i grin at the camera lens in my maternal grandparents' yard.

i lie on my stomach on the bright blanket stretched out on the ground,

obviously for the photo's sake; besides, what would i be doing

in the chicken yard, with the pigsty, geese, the vague

silhouette of the large gate in the background, behind which, blurrily,

wheel-tracks define where the dirt road, here muddy, there dusty,

runs? granted, this last part i add on later, when the photograph turns up

in my hand. but still, what am i doing there? as an adult i will not know

who took the photo, and eventually there will no longer be anyone

who could tell me. maybe my great-aunt's husband? he often comes

on his motorbike from a distant city to my grandparents' house.

there is a chance that it's afternoon in the picture, maybe evening

is falling, but still there is enough light. the photographs of my

early childhood are almost all taken there in my maternal grandmother's

garden, in front of the gate or in the spare room. we will not have

a camera ourselves, but my mother's sister's husband clicks

a few shots of us. in another picture, for instance, in front

of the fence, my father and mother stand—and between them, my happy

child-face. i am held in my mother's arms. we will still look lovely then,

the family i was born into; the weekdays have not yet corroded

my parents too much. at this time they have not yet been corroded

by old age, by cancer.

# Kindergarten

we sit in a circle, in little chairs, there will be a morning story,
*snailywailycomeoutside* and *hidehidegreenbranchgreenleaflet*—
i don't know if i like going to kindergarten. when they take me
there for the first time, i will bellow and cling with all my might
to the door post. later i get used to it, and will be proud of
the bag hanging from my neck, containing the buttered bread with
green peppers, the most delicious ten-o'clock snack. golden-age
flavors: there never was a golden age! a snail will be my sign
over the dressing-room hanger. snaily-waily come outside! later
i don't really remember anything else about that time,
just that we sit in little chairs, the kindergarten teacher is in
a little chair too, and we sing, sometimes we play circle games
and the game where the number of chairs is one less than
the number of children, and when the song arrives at a given word
and we have to sit down, someone will be left without a seat. or two
share one. or a scuffle decides who can push the other aside,
away. on one occasion i don't dare ask permission to go out
to the bathroom, and while we are listening to a story,
i piss, and when it arrives at *andtheylivedhappilyeverafter*
i slink in my now-soaked sweatpants, with a puddle under me.
the teacher notices, and yells at me, and the children surely
burst out laughing. but later i do not remember this,
just that my mother scolds me too. it doesn't matter: my mother
will die anyway, and the kindergarten teacher too. a few years later,

when i run into the teacher or teachers on the street, i no longer
recognize them. i no longer remember their faces, their figures,
if their hair is in a bun, just that sometimes they tell me off
for this or that reason. of my kindergarten classmates, i will just
recall the ones who appear in the photograph taken at the
end-of-year ceremony. we perform the story of the wolf and
the baby goats. i will be one of the seven goats (for the white cap—
maybe bakers wear such things—my mother assembles two long,
conical horns out of drawing paper), in short, i will be one of
the kid goats. in a white shirt, overalls, and a tie i play
my part, and my mother also forces tights on me. because
of this i will surely throw a tantrum, as the others will be
bare-legged. i look stupid enough, as soon as the white
stockings give way, slipping down my shaking knees.
nor will i remember later (but i imagine) what it is like
to stand in the kindergarten courtyard, which barely seems familiar
in the photo, because it's as if there were a little rock garden in it, yet
that doesn't come to my memory, just the sandbox: the plentiful,
yellow sand that the light pours onto, and i stand on the edge
of the sandbox, and don't want to play in it. the teachers then tell
my mother that i am afraid my hands will get dirty. maybe
that's how it will be. i don't know. the sun shines so believably
on the sandbox. everything shines like that! the golden gate
is open. yes. maybe that's it. or maybe the whole thing is just a few
frames of an imagined life?

# Radio

when later i read that in nineteen sixty-three
he was killed, i fail to grasp it fully, since i was then
just a year old. still i remember: one fleeting summer
evening (that is, the november date must be wrong), the radio
announces that kennedy has been shot. the grownups
chatter up a storm, and i return, heart pounding,
to kicking the dust and pebbles. an important thing
has occurred: someone has died, and one can be
shot with a pistol. later i learn that it must be
the other one instead: robert. he is the first
whose death announcement i hear on the radio.
a little man who lives there in the device delivers it,
together with the others, and they relate the news,
and play the tailor family, and sing of course. my father
in those days works at a rental shop, where you can rent
all sorts of things: grinders, tableware (we will have our own)
and radios too. at first we just rent ourselves one,
or else it might be that my father brings it home only
on weekends now and then, and i cannot figure out who
is speaking from the box, and how they fit inside.
according to my parents: tiny dwarf-people. for this reason
i start to fear the radio a little, but it attracts me
all the same. i rotate the knob to issue commands
to the little people. later we purchase an orionton model.

our neighbors, however, have a big electric radio, where
evidently dwarves of larger stature live. and the radio speaks.
the "krónika" show that i call "trónika," and tunes
for dinner at noon, but i don't like that, not nearly as much
as radio novi sad, where a small ship rocks eternally
on the sea of dreams and some request program or other.
and childhood passes by while free europe crackles
in the box too now and then. but i am still small then,
and take no interest in what they say, but only in who
is speaking, and how they lead their lives, and what
they eat, and what clothes they wear, and what kind
of houses they live in, and whether the sun shines there,
and which way the faint breeze blows the boy and girl
on that distant sea, there in that bitch of a box.

# The Legend of Lobo

strip-jointed floor, oil-fired stove, two-hundred seat
auditorium to the world. we always buy tickets for
the twelfth row. the rearmost medium-priced row.
the entrance is five forints. for the first row, two. just once
will i sit up there, to see a soviet film. i have
to keep gazing upwards, my neck starts to hurt,
and the screen will be immense, and the frames will
flicker nervously. there the poor people sit, the proles,
while the six-forint seats are for those who can afford them,
says my father. this places us in society: it classifies us,
separates the extremes. it is less painful to be in the middle.
the mustached, stocky old printer, who always comes
to the movies with his tall, bird-boned wife, regularly
buys tickets for the eleventh row, maybe because
the emergency exits are there, and thanks to the stove
on the right side of the hall, several rows are missing; so,
while watching the film, they can stretch out their legs.
the six-forint tickets sell less. my first motion picture
brings fear to mind. at that time, i do not know that
the wolf running toward the projector will not burst out
of the screen. i am terrified. my parents keep talking
about it long afterward. then i watch the other films:
from blossom time to autumn frost, timur and his squad,
amphibian man, osceola, i see hair there later too. my english-

learning classmates pronounce the title in at least
four different ways. the small town's small high school.
a few jancsó films, the naked migration of women, amarcord:
that widescreen blue pullover, those astonishing breasts:
not desire, not disgust, pure amazement. when i am bigger
and go with my friends to the movies, my favorite spots
will be in rows seventeen and twenty-two. kissing couples,
creaking seats, rattling paper bags. they shoot the godfather,
the oranges tumble and scatter. the buzzing aircraft
of the apocalypse. one time they do not admit minors,
but my classmate, two months my junior, gets in. later
the cinema goes out of business, closes down. i forget
the name of the old cloth-capped projectionist, the stout
cashier lady, whose mouth is eternally painted blood red,
and whose neck has a thick string of pearls looped
around it. when i write this, i look up the legend
of lobo on the internet. i watch it from start to finish.
that is how first love can be.

# Children's Sins

we play bank in the street ditch. we hide our childish valuables
in the drainage ditch pipe—we meaning i, a boy bigger than me,
and two girls. i don't know what we bring there
from home. among the tiny items there is a bright, purple-pink disk
made of aluminum, maybe the cap of some jar, and a few
forgettable, local trifles. later i just remember the pink disk,
and that we tear up grass to disguise the safe, and that
our families yell out to the street to call us home for lunch
from the ditch's late mornings. in the afternoon the band meets up
again, but by now there's no point in turning the grass over,
there's no way anyone will find our treasures in the dry
pipe, since someone ransacked, looted the hiding places.
we'll guess who it could have been. who that thief is
keeping watch as we play. we think our way through a list
of possible perpetrators, we devise plans to bring them down.
one by one we come to suspect every child on the street, one
or two adults too: miska the fool, others. we keep an eye on
the area surrounding the ditch: two boys, two girls, tiny
sherlock holmeses. to see if the criminal returns to the scene.
we investigate for days, but with no result. the suspicion
alone ruins our moods when we make guesses. we do not
accuse each other of theft. maybe it doesn't occur to us that
it could be one of us. later we play different games with

different people. years later the bigger boy and two girls

surely forget the whole thing; the story remains inside me alone,

since the one who steals the treasures from the ditch-safe

is i.

# Cemetery

at first i go with my father to the cemetery, we rarely go.
i am afraid, among the graves, that if i tread on any
spongy or freshly raked little mound of earth,
i will hurt the dead, and god will punish me for it.
away from the herd path, in the old section, we approach
my grandfather's grave. my father will hold my hand as i look
at the carved stone, where another name will be carved too,
without a death date, the name of my grandmother,
who still cooks soup at home, bakes pancakes.
by then the gold on the engraving will be slightly worn,
the light will cast a shadow, which will tumble down
on the surrounding graves, one of which will belong
to an infant, and at the time i will not be able to grasp
how a person can live just three years. my father's father
will then be dead only ten years, and my own father,
when i write this later, over twenty years ago. of course
ten years can be almost as many as twenty years
are few. the past wears down slowly, our lost words
sprout continually from the subconscious. we stand,
my father and i, by his father's grave; at this point
i would go home, but i love the smell of the cemetery,
and if i shut my eyes, i can later evoke that sharp eternal
green fragrance. behind my eyelids the firebugs move,
stuck together in pairs, although it is possible that i just
imagine them over there from the schoolyard, the cracks

in the sidewalk, the vine on our whitewashed house,

that is, from childhood, my childhood, where i stand forever

and ever with my father before his father's grave. my father

takes my hand, and talks, and talks. and sad is the sound

of his voice, and as for my own, i do not know.

# Slipper

at that time i have just turned seven. i will be in the hospital
because i pass out in gym class, yet later i have no memory of this.
let's not even say i regain consciousness. they sent me there for
an examination. but whether those few days will be horrible
or not, i cannot recall after the passing of decades.
the only long moment during the hospital stay that i remember
forty years later is when my slipper gets stuck in the drain.
the children's division will be on the ninth floor; at the end
of the hall the concrete balcony extends into nothing,
and they sometimes let us go there to catch some air.
i don't really remember anything else. i have no
recollection of the hospital food, the dining room,
the nurses, my roommates, the bathroom tile,
the tests, the waiting, the hallway chairs.
nothing, nor whether my parents visit me,
or the color of my pajamas, only that one average
summer evening we stand outside on the balcony
a couple of square meters large, over the town (later
i reconstruct the streets too from my memory, and
the people walking around, bicycling). about the brown
leather slippers i just remember that they are larger
than necessary, probably my parents buy them for
my hospital stay, assuming that i will not
grow out of them right away. even the slipper's
longitudinal seam comes to mind. and that the sides

of the balcony will be made of concrete, and down,

in one corner, a drainpipe opens, through which rainwater

can drain. i put my foot in that hole for fun, and when

i pull it back, i sense that the slightly loose slipper, giving

in to gravity, wants to slip down the sloping drain,

and so visceral anxiety suddenly flows through me,

there, nine floors high. if the slipper does not fall,

i will surely grow into it. but its falling or not falling

becomes unimportant later. just then, in that tense, weeping

moment i believe it must not fall under any

circumstances. i must drag it back with skill somehow:

clench my foot in it, or else bend down for it.

just don't let it fall! since what, what will happen then?

# House

my maternal grandparents will have a sizable porched house
with a spacious closet i like to escape to, the rungs of the ladder
would suit a staircase as well, the attic is free of clutter, yet
full of secrets. an earthen lower kitchen adjoins the house,
and next to it, a huge barn, with swallows' nests under the eaves. when i
am a small child, maybe one or two cows also ruminate inside it, but
it is possible that other cattle pens are projected mistakenly by
the imagination. later, i remember instead the empty manger, and
the cages that will be full of white and black rabbits, for which we have
to gather greens. and then i gather the greens, and the rabbits
chew at an easy pace, and get sick often, and blisters grow on their ears,
around their noses, and then we have to paint them with some kind
of red liquid. but after some time, only chickens scratch around
the yard. at home we will have a concrete room, but my grandparents'
is covered with flooring. i sleep in the room that is unheatable in chilly
weather and winter because it is rarely used; i don't dare stick my feet
out from under the quilt, and not just because of the cold. i am also afraid
of the squeaking floor, the creaking furniture; my grandparents often
tell stories of healers, sorceresses, an old woman for example, who
appears in the evenings as a black dog, and when someone throws
a half-brick at her, the next day he ends up limping. sometimes
my grandfather sends me to fetch water, i should get stronger, because
otherwise i will remain a thin reed. i bring the water back in an enamel
or aluminum jug, and drink out of the lid. my paternal grandmother,

if she saw this, would yell at me, since peasants drink from lids. but
well, my mother's parents are peasants! when decades later i travel again
to the village, the round well will still be there, and i try it out to see
if it still works; the stream of water starts up intermittently, thickly,
a puddle soaks the ground next to the concrete, and thirsty wasps
flicker in the blinding light. later i will overwrite, destroy this picture,
since the well has not yielded water in ages. anyway, when i walk past it,
it will be languid november. where are the wasps at that time? maybe
even in childhood i don't go there for water, but rather aslant down
the road to the pressurized well at the edge of the village; still
the round one adheres better in my memory, since on the way
to and from the bus, which i have to board or get off either at
the iron shop or at the council house farther away, i pass by it. i will be
in high school when my father dies. before then, my grandparents
mostly spend just the summer months at home, and in winters they move in
with their daughter and godfamily. but after the burial we sell the house
with the emptied barn, the attic smelling of dust, the gloomy guest room,
the memories of compotes lined up on the kitchen shelves together with stories
of sorceresses, so that soon the house itself will become a wilderness,
the street too, the village too. so that life itself will grow wild.

# Principal

the principal will come just once to our class.
she will be short, old, ugly, pudgy, and wrinkled moreover.
large earrings will hang from her large ears, thick jewelry
on her neck, and her mouth will be red. she smiles, she speaks
in a honey-glazed voice, the lipstick smears onto
her yellow front teeth, and this makes her look even
dumber. then she says, children, i will ask
you something, and you will answer. how many legs
does a piglet have? four, we resound in unison, to which
she replies in amazement: a cygnet? two! a piglet? four! and
goes on like this for a while. she marvels: what silly kids
you are! you didn't even know how many legs a cygnet has?!
the teacher smiles, and we smile, the principal is so
funny. but maybe we do this only out of solidarity
because our teacher is smiling too. or maybe we're just
giving ourselves some relief, since the principal
has scared us a little. or something like that. finally
the class will burst out laughing, the teacher and principal
too—why, how happily the sixties go by! and yet
restlessness makes a nest in the great merriment. just a
moment passes, barely a nest's straw, and it gets entangled
with a tiny, white-throated anxiety, an awareness that
the principal is free to do anything: be strict and humorous,
yell when she feels like it, and if it's to her liking, smile,

and lord it over us with her cygnets and piglets,

and we always have to adjust our behavior

to the teacher, the principal, adults in general.

later, when i grow up, i myself start playing the principal's

silly games with my sons when they are little,

and they laugh and get mad at the same time,

and i cunningly keep switching the consonants

until we tire of it. is it possible that my children see

me as a capricious adult, the same way i see the principal

forty years deeper in poem-time, one autumn

afternoon? later i think about how the principal

was a child once herself. finally this also occurs

to me: all of her aging is in vain, since surely

there are people who mess with her too.

# Waiting

it would be good if it were november and we were awaiting guests
for my mother's or grandmother's name day. katalin and elizabeth
are close in the calendar. it would be twilight, the sky would be gray
and vast, those few snow clouds would be lost in it. i would climb up
the bare, old mulberry tree and look around the world, but would see
just into the neighbors' gardens, up to their houses. inside, a goose
would be baking in a cast-iron pot, its smell heavy and good, and i
would know that the liver is all for me. a twenty-five-watt bulb
lights up the kitchen's few square meters, much more brightly
than the petroleum lamp a few years ago. i would love the bulb's
rare light, the way it keeps the shivering secrets in the corners of
the room. or the way the darkness slowly swells on the room's
open door. at the kitchen table i would play with toy soldiers,
like the ones my sons play with later, except that they will have
many more. i would have three, among them a yellow one,
a machine-gunner, helmeted and kneeling, whose gun-barrel
i would cut with an antler-handled knife, and afterwards regret
cutting, since time will not glue it back together again.
this same antler-handled knife, which my grandfather made
even before my birth, my grandmother would shortly use to cut
the goose liver. the liver's outside would be brown and crunchy,
the inside yellow and soft, but i would prefer the fried shell. it
could also be the case that there is no name day this time (since
we cut up a goose every week, besides slaughtering a pig),

and that no guests are coming. it is also possible that outside,
in tiny flakes, snow begins to fall, and also that only
christmas will be white. or not even that.
at that time almost everything would still be possible. time
would not yet be written.

# Long Underwear

at the school i will attend, the stoker will be a mustached
old man. we always see him wearing a cloth cap, blue
apron. he comes in during lessons too. he doesn't knock, just
opens the door, takes care of things, shovels coal from the bucket
into the iron furnace, whose door sometimes emits smoke,
sometimes coal gas too. at such times the teacher tells
one of the boys: open the window! and then we will freeze, but once
the room is ventilated, the huge stove surrounded by a
protective grille heats up quickly, and we sweat in the classroom.
at that time changing into slippers will not be in fashion yet.
the floor is oily, and we boys mostly go around in hunting boots.
the soles of these boots are leather, and i like the sound
of the iron toes as they knock on the sidewalk, like the noise
of footsteps in old films. with such tough shoeing you can give
someone a terribly painful kick in the shin. we pull thick jaeger
socks into the boots, the upper part of which are folded over
the footwear in several layers, but sometimes we wrap
foot cloths on thin socks. we have to do this with skill, because
if we roll the fabric badly, it will move away, and it will
cause discomfort, pinching the foot. under our pants we slip
long underwear. there will be two kinds: one is the jaeger,
which i prefer to the traditional kind, whose legs must be
attached at the bottom with two laces. the badly tied underwear
sticks out of the math teacher's pants in summer too, whereas i

hate wearing long underwear even in winter, though outside it

clearly serves a good purpose; yet later i will no longer recall

what it felt like to wear them, just that when, on the first and

chilly day of spring, i beg not to have to wear them, that already

is freedom. the lenten wind blows into the sweatpants,

or just flutters my clothes back and forth on my thighs,

and sensually touches my down-soft skin. on the first spring day

without long underwear i have an intoxicating tingling feeling,

but afterwards i get used to it, and new winters, new long

underclothes are needed, so that, escaping from them,

i can be free again, while time's fabric, slowly wearing,

tears apart—and cannot be sewn into existence.

# Chickenshit

nestling chicks can chirp in such a way that the ears
almost hurt. it will be springtime, with trickling eaves, indoors
the stove is hot—or not! it will be april weather,
when the broody hatches chickens in the chamber.
the broody's body will be hot, and she taps my hand with her beak
if i reach out to her. my grandmother sometimes shines a light
on the eggs, looking to see if something will become of them or
they have rotted. the chicks stay caged in a corner of the kitchen
until they grow strong. at first we slice up cooked eggs
for them, later they eat grist. when i get bigger, i have
to grind it. fluffy, yellow weightlessnesses! someone steps
on one of them, another one gets its brains crushed by the sow,
or the cat grabs one from the brood. but most of them grow up,
i will have a favorite among them. i give the bald-necked one a name.
then a couple of years later my grandmother slaughters it too.
she heats the plucking water, sharpens the knife. i will then
have to catch the chosen roosters, chicks, chickens. she tears
their necks a little, and cuts them off. my mother likewise.
only my father turns away and does not look in our direction
when his mother or his wife slaughters poultry. i don't dare
kill the chickens either, but i watch anyway as they writhe,
their legs twitch, they fend off that strangeness with their wings.
sometimes they get away, they wriggle out of my mothers' hands,
they stagger with dangling head, before a soup or paprika dish

is made of them. i do not eat their meat gladly. the smell of
plucked feathers takes away my appetite. nor do i like the smell
of henhouses: the odor of their shit-covered roosts, the dust
that the roosters and chicks stir up with their wings and that sticks
to the nose and throat. sometimes they are lice-infested too,
then we sprinkle lice-killer under their wings, between their feathers,
into the chicken coop. every morning my grandmother feels
the hens for eggs. they say that if someone touches the hens' bottoms
to sense whether an egg can be expected that day, that person knows
how many to look for in the nests and elsewhere. i collect all
the eggs. sometimes i fold the hens' heads under their wings,
i rotate them, and then they stay motionless for a few minutes.
like carcasses, they lie on the ground. and i run to my grandmother,
come quickly, look what happened: they died. then she scolds me,
chases me, wielding whatever she happens to grab: a broom,
a shovel. but i will be quick, whereas her gait is bent. the hens
shit the yard all over. we keep stepping into the watery crap,
then wiping our shoes. i will hate the chicken yard. later
my mother will keep fewer chickens, just a few, but those ones
shit too. then when she slaughters the last one, i will not notice
that i no longer have to clean my shoes after them. besides,
i come home less and less often. and i will be unaware that
the lack that scratches inside me has anything to do
with the chickens.

# Carcass Well

as long as i am growing up, the forest at the end of our garden
also grows up, from seedlings; pheasants run this way and that
among the trees, sometimes wild rabbits too, but most of the time
just chickens, escaping from the yard, scratch all sorts of crawling
things out of the soil. behind the little forest, toward the cemetery,
there will be an older poplar thicket, where the trunks, the leaves, even
the shadows are darker. i never go that way to the cemetery,
only to the well. near the well, the planted poplar forest
comes to an end. in the clearing the sun always shines, and enormous
willow and greengage plum trees border the other side. that part
will be recessed (an old adobe pit), and after heavy showers
the fluttering grass billows under the gathering lukewarm water.
the carcass well will be somewhere behind the bushes, close to
the lonely house of the dogcatcher. the dogcatcher is not lonely, he has
a mother, a wife, blond children. i on the other hand will be
alone, when i look down onto the billowy meat-pile in the well.
the well is not a true well, its diameter is too wide for that.
but when i am an adult the memorable humming remains in my
sound-recollection, because there will be an abundance of flies:
their abdomens zigzag green and blue. and it will be very smelly
there. i don't dare take a breath, instead i run away, and
at a distance, like a diver, inhale, filling my lungs with
enough oxygen for the next sneak peek.
when i write this, i will remember that the carcass well

breathes, that the carcass well's animals breathe,

the animals whose corpses are ordered by the veterinarian

to be destroyed. the nearby meat factory also feeds the well,

and the meats, the skins, the furs, the rotting interiors

billow in a heap. the worms billow in the carcasses, the whole

blanket of being billows, and my stomach turns, as i think

about the essence of the sight. in the midst of my writing

it occurs to me that the associations with baudelaire's carcass

and horror stories might be the only things billowing,

and my stomach too, since after each batch of corpses

they sprinkle the well with chlorine. nor do i know

what will happen to the well if it fills up. will they bury it

and dig a new one, like graves next to graves? reality can be overwritten:

my stomach billows, like grass underwater, and

the text settles in the immaculate sunshine.

# Dread

we will have singing class, with revolutionary songs;
outside, in the sloppy late winter or early spring, under the chilly,
low sky i go home. my mother is cooking now, and i look
into the larder where my grandmother lives. or should i
say rather, into my grandmother's room? the compotes,
the lard-tubs are kept there too, one of them full of roasted
pork sides, and apples are lined up there on the shelves,
they wrinkle all winter in a diminishing collection, and
at winter's end they're all dotted with rot, at that point only
good for applesauce. so anyway, i take a peek into
my grandmother's room. my grandmother is lying on
her bed, on her back, though it is humped. i would
marvel that she does not roll onto her side, but instead
of marveling, i am scared, because she is lying with
her mouth open, and she is not snoring, not even
breathing. i go up close to her, and i know it:
she has died. outside the flat, rainy sky, indoors the iron
stove is still hot, there is gelatinous dread in my heart. i keep
an eye on my grandmother. i count how many years she lived,
and tremble. in the kitchen my mother asks what's wrong.
i go out to the yard, roam around there, and then come back
to grandma. i look, go out, come back in again. meanwhile
my father comes home, but i say nothing to him about
his mother dying. i might be eight. or nine. i never saw

a dead person before. grandma's face is wrinkled, mouth
agape. she has just one broken front tooth, a tooth-stump.
it is not as if i would see it, i would just know. but
what a pretty young woman she is in the wedding picture,
sixty years earlier! it will be quiet, as in the photograph.
outside springtime skulks, inside the apples are rotting.
and sometimes in secret i steal a jar of preserves and gobble it
all up at once. but this time the preserves don't even
cross my mind. i go outside, i go back in, i listen.
i wait for something to happen: for my parents to notice
that grandma has died. or do they already know? the hours
go by, the dread stays constant. maybe i get used to it by
and by, but still keep thinking about *it*. then, once, when again
i take note of my grandmother, how she is not breathing,
that one time she just opens her eyes and asks: what time is it,
my little boy? it will be startling, like a horror film. of course
at that point i don't know yet that horror films exist. a miracle,
that i don't die of fright! afterwards, childhood passes by,
i grow up, but grandma does not get older, since there's no
way to get more bent, no room on her skin for more wrinkles,
but she still grumbles away with us for fifteen years or so.
and when she dies, i do not look at her face on the bier.

# Uncle Doctor

*uncle doctor is a blessed* man. he wears gold-rimmed
lennon glasses, and his hair is like jimmy hendrix's.
just blond-brown. they even badmouth him for it, which
is natural in a small town at that time. but he is known
as a good doctor, and that makes people overlook
his hippie vibe. he will have whiskers too, and blue
eyes, if i remember that detail well so many years later,
when i write this. all in all he stays a couple of years
in the village. whether he himself wants to go elsewhere, or
whether the place still has not accepted him, i don't know,
since i will be a child when he moves away, yet nonetheless
he remains the one that the *sick little* boy remembers, decades
later, as good uncle doctor. at that time i have been lying
in bed for days, or maybe not that long, just the fever
holds on more stubbornly than usual, and my parents
call for the doctor. it would be so good to write: *obscurity*
*gently lines the fur* of his coat draped over the hanger,
but it will be summer, sunshiny, hot, and i rot
feverishly under the duvet. (let's say i move all
the feathers toward my feet, so just the case covers me.)
the heat doesn't want to go down further. i could be
ten or twelve by then. i will have no desire or strength
for reading. the fever relaxes, it even dampens my fear
of death, although it cannot drive it away entirely. and

then he arrives, bends over me. shaggy hair, glasses
flashing encouragement. the stethoscope is cool compared
to me. i shiver, but that is already good shivering. it's possible
that uncle doctor's finger *knocks* a little *on my skinny ribs,*
i don't recall it later. just that he prepares an injection:
he draws the liquid into the syringe and, holding it toward
the light, squeezes one or two sagging drops from
the needle. i don't know whether it's the serum that actually
heals me, or whether it's uncle doctor's overflowing calm.
yet i feel better right away. my grandmother also notices
as she pulls the sweaty cover over the bedding. maybe i ask
for food, maybe i start to read, maybe i ponder the platitudes
of life and death a little, maybe i think of my jimmy hendrix
with lennon glasses too, but it does not enter my imagination
that he *makes his way to the theater or has dinner in silence.*
only later does kosztolányi's *poor little child* occur to me.
true, in my illness, at that time, i would not think of my doctor
in the context of theater or dining at home; at most i would
picture a canteen lunch: in a school or farmers' cooperative
cafeteria.

# Bag of Straw

the stubble is bright, the yellow smell might stay forever
inside my nose, just like the smell of piss. with bales taken home
from the wheat fields in summer we fill the bags to the brim.
the used, crumbled straw of last year we dump onto the garbage heap,
the chickens scratch it apart. the newly filled bag of straw
will be tall and soft. it crunches quietly, as the stems move
around when i throw myself onto it, into the tender sinking.
the room fills up with a yellow, bright fragrance, and it lasts
a couple of days, as long as i do not wet my pants. i am
a schoolchild by then, but i still do it. sometimes daily,
at one point not for a month, then i wake up to find heat
pouring onto my loins, and another time, if i kick off my covers,
my piss is cold, sticky slush. that is when i pull a duvet over me,
and wait, motionless, to warm up and fall asleep. under the sheet
there is protective plastic, of course. i hate it because it rattles.
no matter what. if i toss and turn, my mother wakes up
to the rustling, she will get suspicious, she'll ask what's
the matter, she will take the pissy sheet out from under me, give
me a dry one, dry nightclothes too, and sometimes with a big fuss,
or hell knows why, she starts washing in the middle of the night.
i just blink in the not-too-strong but still painful lamplight
emanating from the bare, fly-beshat bulb. that's how she punishes me.
sometimes she washes in silence, sometimes grumbling, sometimes
yelling. she's so sorry, so sorry for herself. going back to sleep
in the dry bedding is not easy, if the conscience is damp.

# Public Baths

the buffet will have bambi orange soda and fried dough. flies and wasps
are humming. and forty years later—on a foggy november day, when
the light is on in my room before noon—the summer bath atmosphere
will flutter in, and i will remember it as it unfolds: little boys and girls
making noise, while the bigger ones sunbathe with lazy desire
on the gray-painted edge of the swimming pool. the soft eroticism
of all spas hovers above the waters. farther along, tired heavy bodies
in the thermal bath known as the foot-corn-soaker: surgical scars,
varicose veins, fat and skinny people, i look at them, a flat-chested
child in gym shorts, and am disgusted by the flabby ladies' white
skin or the freckled backs burnt to a roast, and by the fact that
someone always pees into the water, and yet i sink in it up to
my neck, and later do not understand why something that is bad
can be good. the white disc of the sun is beating into the tall sky
of afternoon. it burns. heat, sweat, ripe melon pulp. in one of
the pools the water is lukewarm, in the other, piss-warm. slipshod,
lazy conversations, gossip, children's squeals. a racket of splashes,
splatters. some loudspeaker is crackling. wasps buzz and words
do too. in the water's mirror, the tiniest movements break
the lightweight, white clouds into pieces.
and the water will have an odor. an odor.

# Chess

by late morning the sun no longer reaches the front
of the east-facing house. i sit in the shade at the base
of the whitewashed wall and try to immerse myself
in some chess manual, but with no luck. my father
does not play chess, so where he works as a store
apprentice, he asks the master to teach me. uncle lajos
presses two small books into my hands, so that i
may read them and then we may play. but i cannot
find my way into the explanations of the moves,
the opening theories, the game descriptions. i go
unprepared to my first lesson, but nonetheless
learn the rules quickly. later we play many games.
uncle lajos is a kind man, he often smiles. at least
his eyes do. and he explains and expounds. on all kinds
of topics: the kakat backwaters, mills, carpentry,
the shop that once was theirs, the old city, the old
people, italy, where his son lives. in the door
of the former store facing the crossroads, rolling
tin blinds are eternally drawn. when i come over
to play chess, new families have already moved
into their corner house, and they have only one flat.
a policeman lives in the house, and a shoemaker too,
apparently in peace. uncle lajos's wife is descended
from a baron soldier; i will soon beat her at chess.

uncle is the tougher opponent, yet sometimes
i manage to defeat him, even though i fall short
in the final score. i like to go to their place. they offer
me cake. everything is more beautiful there. at home
a simple lampshade covers the bulb, like next door,
but here they light their room with a chandelier.
and the chairs, beds, cabinets ... everything
holds more elegance and ornament; the pictures
on the wall, the wall pattern too, and the patina cups.
several pieces are missing from the chess set, though,
and later i no longer remember which ones. a bishop
for sure. a knight, some pawns? uncle lajos carves
new ones, and paints them nicely too. still they differ
from the rest. on the bishop the ochre looks rougher,
less polished. of course that does not interfere with
the game itself. or does it? now the world is no longer
flawless. just as plate and drinking glass sets diminish,
just as the house gets turned into apartments, ancestors
into a family tree, and their remains get scattered,
so the bishop and other pieces fall away, out of sight.
who knows where and how? later i will have my own
chess set and will play with the boy from next door
in the shady late mornings on the summer veranda. then
he falls away too. or i fall away. or we just move.
my own chess set will still be complete when i write this,
but the house on the corner will be torn down by then.
the land will be exactly like the site of a house freshly
demolished, and a light bishop, maybe the ochre-

painted one, maybe the original, like a useless
archaeological find, may be rotting there somewhere
under the mound of earth, the brick debris.

# Garden

forty years later i will be able to list the garden's trees:
two quince trees by the street fence, one plum tree, which
the grapevine climbs onto, and from which we pick the sweet,
thick-skinned othello grapes. then the old cherry tree.
how often i climb it! three sour cherry trees, and again
plum, apple, turkish hazelnut, and if at the foot of the garden
we turn around by the gooseberry and raspberry bushes:
two summer apple trees, one with fruit that is sweet
and red-striped, and if i shake it, the seeds inside it rattle,
the cats are forever eyeing the birds living in the hollow
of the trunk. the other one bears green, tart apples,
my grandmother calls them vinous. further along, between
the well and the house, scraggly little pear and peach trees
probe the soil and their chances of survival until
one by one they dry up. the mulberry and elder trees
stand in the yard; a tall rosebush, directly in front
of the house. hosts of little pink flowers burst out
of the buds. they are beautiful at the time, but my mother
does not like them, because they wilt quickly, and she
cannot deal with sweeping all the withered, browned
petals that fall on the veranda. the rosebush is in bloom
one summer when my father nails a fence plank that
has gone loose. the hammer does not suit his hand, his father's
smith-machinist tools (huge pinchers, keys) are rusting

in the attic, but still he teaches me how to hold the nail,

how to strike it without hitting our hands, and maybe

he accidentally hits his own, but that is not why

his eyes get misty. he solemnly says: see, when i am

here no more, this is how you hold the hammer.

# Knife-throwing

auntie juliska will not be smelly, but she won't have a good odor either.
and how scared she is, poor thing! when a knife flits right in front
of her face and, just a few centimeters from her, fixes its point
in the portico column, and vibrates a little with its own momentum.
i have to practice a lot before i learn such a mighty throw that can
brazenly plunge the old mud-cleaning blade or stolen kitchen knives
into the mulberry's thick trunk, next to the outhouse, from four or five
meters away. i pinch the blade between my index finger and thumb
and estimate the the distance. i feel the power of the throw.
the kids next door and i play indians. some of them sometimes steal
their father's secret air rifle, we shoot at empty tin cans; another time
we try our skill with a u-nail slingshot, a pointed arrow. once we even
bring a washtub into the sizable adobe pit, where water accumulates
at raintime; we glide by canoe between the poplars, or, more accurately,
push ourselves with sticks in the water that goes up to a child's knees,
and we steer our basin toward the ad hoc goal, where a few years later
in early fall my father cuts our fourth neighbor down from the tree. when i
arrive home from school, i get scared, because the police are questioning
my father. but three days later, i look terrified at the young man
in the beret who leans on their plank fence, a thick white
bandage around his neck. he is smiling. then the story could already
be turning out well (of course, what is well?) but a few months later,
no one cuts him down. his teenage daughter, who will later attend school
laughing with her girlfriend, will be an orphan. and auntie juliska will be quite

an orphan too! her face gets even wrinklier than my grandmother's.
she is a tall, stooped old woman, who goes around in dark clothes,
in an apron. she will not have children, relatives, she enters into
a housing contract, with a family with many children,
and they quarrel a lot!—those kinds of contracts always lead
to trouble! then afterwards she no doubt dies too. i have no idea
when or of what. later i don't remember her face either, just her wrinkles,
and that she will have the odor of an old person. not good,
not smelly either. stuffy rather. we think of auntie juliska as
a crazy old lady, we street kids. and we treat her as such, with
insolence. but she is just old, and lives alone; she is helpless around
the mocking kids. the grownups get mad at us when we take
advantage of her. my grandmother gives me a few slaps; though she
is old, she carries her years well. auntie juliska will be long dead
when my grandmother mentions reproachfully that i hurled the knife
into the column in front of the unlucky old woman's nose.

# Embezzlement

before easter, we would stand gaping at the shooting-range that has been moved
onto the market square; the carousel spins the riders higher than the crowd—
or not. no one's there but the fairground technicians, who come every year
at this time to our village and are now setting up. on the display sticks
all sorts of things shine: dolls, medals, keychains,
decks of cards offer themselves. before this i would never shoot
a rifle, whose vizier and barrel are altered so that
you can hit the target only by accident. my parents would at least
discuss this at home, as if this were important to them, but maybe
they just say it so that i may learn the skew of the world,
how to calculate the probability of luck. we would be wearing
school uniforms, we ten-year-old boys with bangs;
we would want to hit our target like the indians in films and
the heroes in prewar penny-booklets about the underworld,
and we would believe that the underworld is under the earth,
and damp, winding, carnal-smelling tunnels lead to such cities
as we have hereto only seen in movies. we want so badly
to shoot that it occurs to us that a pouch of money is rattling in
my bag, since i have to collect class money for some collection. maybe
a shot costs five forints. i would shoot one, then another one or two.
of course they would all miss, and my classmates would like to shoot
too, but i wouldn't give them money, for which they
would chase me. decades later i would remember myself
running out of the market square, with the unbuttoned school uniform

waving above me, and with each step the handful of coins ringing

menacingly in the pouch, and my heart hammering loudly

and nervously. but they wouldn't catch up. afterwards i would cajole

a few forints out of my parents, yet they would ask what i needed

it for, and when i admitted that i shot away a portion of the class

money, they would replace it, but first would give me

a few slaps. or maybe they wouldn't slap me. when i

write this, i no longer remember.

# Scissors

my grandmother will have other scissors too: smaller, larger,
sharper—but most of all i will love the pair that has, below
the rings, on the wide-opening, ornate handle-necks,
the likenesses of a man and woman embossed. they have
been looking at each other for a hundred years. the man
from the left, the woman from the right. you can no longer pinpoint
their features; the portraits are tiny anyhow, but my grandmother
claims that they are franz joseph and sisi. of course she will say
queen elisabeth, and from behind her broken spectacles
her aged eye contemplates the heads with their worn lines,
which i wear down even more, whenever i polish them
with sandpaper. later i do not remember whether my grandmother,
as a young woman, still in the time of the monarchy, was given
the scissors or bought them, but as a child i listen to the heaps
of tales she happily tells. about everything. she tells of her
husband, a smith-mechanic, and of my father's sister, jolanka,
who died of dysentery at age twelve. my father was only six then,
he survived. and my grandmother tells of the coronation too—
when they still live in pest—of charles and zita. she speaks
reverently of the king's wig, i cut something with the scissors,
and franz joseph's and elisabeth's portraits come close
with each clip, but they never touch. only the rings make
a metal clap, and the blades scrape, and then the past
dissolves in the future, and then they bury my grandmother,

and i forget her stories, all i remember about them is their

having been, and only the scissors remain, and

the sewing box with the thimble, then the thimble vanishes too.

the scissors i have sharpened though, and now i have them

on my desk as i write this, and i look at the king and queen,

whose unhappiness has long dissolved in their shared lore,

the books, films, the portrait-bearing schönbrunn souvenirs.

i click the scissors as a child, then as an adult, if i need to cut

something or open an envelope, and i love them, but i take no

interest in the royal figures, having no interest in the question

of power or of birthplace either. this cannot be quite

correct. i should disambiguate this *havingnointerest,*

and explain why not. i should gradate the assertions

and misgivings: polish them, sand them. in any case,

all embellishment wears away, and only the man

remains, and the woman: faces on a pair of scissors,

unhappy peacetime.

# Fathers

when i am ten i will see my father as an aged
man. in daily life he will walk around toothless,
sunken-faced. he will put on his dentures only
for holidays, i will grin at them then, and he will
also laugh. he is a born clown, but if he forgets
himself, he can get emotional too. he rarely does.
he recovers from tb, but not from stomach and
heart disease. yet he makes it to seventy-five,
in fact a day past. he bicycles until his cancer, while
inventing the beard in a nearly well-shaven world.
actually i would like a younger father, a different one,
because i will often be ashamed of him. as if he could
not be taken seriously by serious people who carry sacks,
stab the porker themselves, and in the mornings,
on their way to work, pour at least half a shot down
their throats, and strut around in the kind of clothes that
normal workers can be seen wearing in textbooks. and who
do not scold the system, at least not in front of me. nor will
my father be a soldier—true, nor will i be one later, somehow
i work things out—but in my childhood i still consider it
a grave deficiency that my father cannot append his own story
to military history, whereas i still have an imaginary future
as a cowboy and a partisan, who knows no fear and who

handles the light colt revolver and heavy machine gun
with great skill. one of my classmates brags that
his father is a corporal, at which another shoots back
that his is a captain, and another trumps them with colonel,
but i know that his father rides a luggage bike around,
a drunk young room-painter in a beret cannot be
a colonel, and i call him a liar, since i still don't know
how sensitive we are about our lies. my father is sensitive
as well. when he reads on my first report card that he
is a night guard, for half an afternoon he quarrels with
my mother because she did not dictate: storekeeper. he will
be proud that even before the war he learned the profession.
but when they give him disability status, he chooses to be
a porter, which at that time people refer to as: day guard,
night guard. my father looks down on night guards, my father
looks down on many people and badmouths them. maybe
he looks down on himself too, as his clothes get shabbier
and shabbier, the weekdays soil his elegant suits. a mixture
of hippie and homeless. he knows everything better than
everyone else. that is how he rebels. he collects manias
and empty bottles. he does not redeem the latter, and
when he dies, i collect beer bottles by the hundreds from
the garden weeds. he used to soak the labels
off them in a basin, and he must have stowed them
away somewhere, but i cannot find those. my father
will win the lottery in his dreams. yet he is entirely sane.
he survives typhus, tuberculosis, a war, communism. sometimes

i am ashamed of my father. sometimes i am proud
of him. and soon i realize that in many ways
i will come to resemble him.

# Earth

the soil will be soft, but it will not stick. the iron will glide,
shining into the black earth. but turning it over will be
difficult, since i always scoop a larger piece than i should,
so that the work will go more quickly. truly i would rather
not dig, except to get the whole thing done with. to say
that i dug up the garden. that would be so grown up.
but my parents would assume that i strained myself,
that i will get a hernia or something of that sort.
the springtime creaks when the spade turns pieces of
gravel or shards up out of the ground, the shiny
earthworms, cut in two, wriggle their way drooling
out of the damp lumps, and in their routes of passage,
time doubles. years come when moles threaten
the vegetable crop. they keep turning up tiny pieces
of earth from their fresh rootings, and sometimes i
stick a fork into them, but never manage to stab
even one little purblind animal. nonetheless
i sometimes find dead specimens in the garden.
i would have no idea how they come out of their
little caves to wither in the sun, like weeds
that have been hoed out. sometimes we bury
a dog, baby kittens in the earth. other times
i go searching for treasure. i would be satisfied
with old coins from the avar or kuruc era. but

most of all i would like to find weapons: pistols,
machine guns, wrapped and lubricated, which the
wounded russian and german soldiers abandoned
in the second world war. if only someone had buried
them. but only bits of rusty iron turn up, which
in no way resemble weapons' remains. in the
area you also come upon mysterious mounds,
known as kunhaloms, inside which, supposedly,
illustrious lords were buried at some time or other.
in the neighboring village, near my grandparents'
house, there will be an acacia-covered mound
with one side lopped off, in which, according to
the locals, the bones of an old king lie, surrounded
by who knows how many treasures. nevertheless
the villagers do not break apart the mound of earth,
but in a few decades i will no longer be able to find it.
it will be bulldozed away and replaced with a gas station.

# Discoveries

the white man's way—let that be the title of the book that i
read at that time. in the evenings, in winter. at the kitchen table.
a twenty-five-watt bulb lights the area under the lamp bespattered
with flies. though it is possible that my mother cleans them away
in autumn, and there will be no fly-splatter for winter. if we are
cooking, it will be hot, the stovetop sometimes turns red, but then
the kitchen quickly goes cold. the chill comes through the never-
insulated door. but it doesn't bother me. i sail with scurvied sailors
to discover parts of the world that lie on spicy, warm seas, to kill
the rapturous natives for the sake of glass beads. with diaz i round
the cape of good hope, with vasco da gama i make it to india, with
magellan i die on a faraway island, with the conquistadors i kill
indians, with captain cook i seek a passageway, and i find
australia, i freeze on a dogsled on an arctic expedition, i travel to inner
africa to warm up—but i will always be a white man. the book is heavy,
with large-scale, yellowed, but luminous peacetime pages,
engravings here and there, and silken pages before the engravings.
my father browses it too, he takes it out with him on duty now and then,
and once his boss asks him for it and does not give it back.
as an adult i plan for a long time to go seek out
the site manager and ask for the book back, yet
i never do it. in the meantime i begin to read books
of a different sort; and with cooper-novels
i become an indian.

# Rag Soccer

back in those days i am hanging out with the neighborhood kids.
we band together: street locals. a few of us are a couple of years
younger, others a few years older. girls too get mixed into
the team, but rarely will there be as many of us as when
we go outside after a rain to play soccer in the pasture, where
the spots of puddles can barely be seen from the grass. only
when we step in them does the warmed water splash forth
its presence. for the goal, a few half-bricks from the nearby ditch banks
will suffice, maybe twigs sharp enough to stick in the ground;
we might even throw a shirt on each of them, to make
them easier to see. we will have a rag ball, sopping wet.
nonetheless, when i write this, i lose all certainty that it really
is like this, or my memory just conjures the archaic ball sewn
out of rags instead of a spotted rubber ball. i try to probe deeper, but
i only touch a colorless, wet rag-object—in those days,
on those streets, in any of our childhoods, receiving a hide ball
is almost unheard of, but the rubber one, one degree worse,
is rare too. anyway, it gets spattered by the puddles in the grass
in the cow-dungy, mushroomy meadow; our feet and soles
spatter it too. among us there will be one disabled boy,
he will have deformed feet, he cannot stand on them, he strides
with his hands, he just drags his vestigial lower limbs along,
like an animal with an injured hind leg. according to the doctors,
he will die soon. but he survives the forecast considerably,

and later, as a big teenager, gets a three-wheeled mobility bike,
which he can drive himself. in summer you can often see
his half-naked, muscular trunk. he resolutely rolls
the handpedal the length of the street and farther, even throughout
the '80s. but when we play soccer after a rain, we know
that he will die soon and that there will be no more bicycle.
on all fours, soaked to the skin, he pushes and pulls himself
after the rag ball one carefree twilight on the summer
lawn: he reaches forward with his hands, quickly, quickly,
and then pulls his body: he is allowed to touch the ball
with his hand, to kick it with his hand. when forty years later
i return to my home there, which by now will not be my home,
at one corner a wheelchaired man of my age, possibly he,
suddenly turns my way. we greet each other, just as strangers do
on the deserted streets of small villages. at the time of
our short encounter i do not notice his feet, but as soon as we
pass each other, i turn back, in case it might be he.
it might be the neighbor boy too! from behind i can no longer
identify him. and if it were he—what of it? memory
will erase him soon, the memory will soon be erased.

# Bread

through the pits i would head homeward from the baker's, where
there is always a good smell and so many people that sometimes
i would stand in the courtyard and the line would spill out to the street.
the baker is tall, thin, bald, mustached, and bespectacled, but i
would rarely see him, since his wife would be the one serving,
the smiling plump woman, who would cut the huge breads with
a huge knife. she would affably swing the round-edged
bread slicer, and her mouth wouldn't stop for a second, she
would chat with the local men and women, whose waists
would be all i could see in line, or their backs, the worn-out rags
they would wear when pouring hogwash onto the pigs
one morning at the turn of the sixties and seventies. at that time
the news would tell of the vietnam war, and i would
dread the thought of the americans dropping an atom bomb
on our necks, and of what would happen then; if my parents
started speaking of politics, someone would always cut in:
keep it down! or else: not in front of the child! it would be
eternally hot at the bakery, especially in summer. but in winter
i would also sweat in my coat while standing in line, and
the lady would slip the still-steaming, three-kilo loaf into
my mesh bag. i would go home through the pits—the adobe
was taken from there to the houses in the new part of town
fifty years earlier. i would head homeward between the scrubby
poplars, which would later grow up with me. in rainy weather

going through the pits would not be allowed, on account of
the mud. i must avoid them as i head for the pavement,
but nonetheless i take a shortcut sometimes, and then
at home they scold me for my muddy shoes. however,
on that particular morning, when i head home with the bread,
the yellow clay mud will be frozen, it will be winter, january,
because in january we always kill, and so we will have
slaughtered pork at home, a big mess of it. i get up when it
is still dark, the scorching pork hums in the dawn, and the boiling
water, which we pour onto the pig, soaks up the frozen earth, and
there will be mud in the yard, slightly bloody mud. later i
head home through the pits, the young, hoarfrosting poplars
dissolve farther away in the thin fog under the fog-gray
sky. i pick at the bread's shiny, brown, fragmented shell
more and more impatiently, more and more hungrily,
and by the time i get it home, i have eaten a chunk of it.
they scold me for this, but not a lot—my mother also
loves the warm crispy edge. maybe she talks about the bread's
holiness as well, but she doesn't draw a cross on it before
breaking it. i think only my maternal grandmother
used to draw one, but i rarely see her, and when i grow up,
i will no longer remember whether she did this routinely
or just showed me once how they used to do it long ago.
it is mainly the limping singing teacher who talks about
the holiness of bread, she who always compares the kingdom
of hungary to a beautiful three-kilo loaf, even draws it on
the board, and we hear from her mouth once: broken-hungary.
she also recites a poem that calls it heaven. she wears

thick-framed glasses too, like the baker, her voice will

be strong, and she keeps such order that you can hear

a fly buzzing in the classroom while she speaks, and then

she gives such slaps that the mouth of some child called up

to answer for some misdeed will crack, blood will start

running from his nose, and he stumbles, knocking

over the seats. when i grow up later, i do not understand

how, in the seventies, she could go on about "broken hungary"

with impunity, or how, with impunity, she could beat

children bloody. i am a good child, just once i end up

getting punished, because during the break i stayed indoors

and this is against the rules. but in fact i didn't

stay inside, the reporting student would just write a few of us up

out of malice, and before class we would line up for a slap,

and the beast of a singing teacher would not ask, just hit,

and i, the spoiled only child, would quickly come to learn

that i am just like anyone else: i can get in trouble for rubbish,

i can be beaten without cause.

# Homeroom Teacher

in fifth grade we get a new homeroom teacher. a fortyish, bald
man. there will be no *pointed hat* on his head, the remainder of
his hair falls in long brown curls, blue *eyes pure as a lake*, his nose
will be slightly large, his given name is unusual. he recounts
that besides himself, he knows of three people who received
this name (among them one of the heroes of a jókai novel).
he teaches biology and drawing. then we will already have a drawing
display board, and must affix the sheet onto it somehow. he sells
the tacks for twenty pennies but tells me, you don't have to pay.
we buy honey from him. somehow he and my father
become friends, but the first family visit occurs in a rather
strange manner. that year the homeroom teacher moves from
carpathian ruthenia to our village; however, his wife is allowed
to follow him only a year later. they rent a peasant's house
near the school, a kitchen, two rooms overcrowded with
relatively antique furniture, which they bring along from
their former home. they will not have children. many times
i go over to their place. the wife is russian born, later
i forget her name, but will never forget her slightly angular,
neither beautiful nor ugly face. and her voice stays in my ears,
the way it sputters russian, breaks hungarian. i go to see them
because she is a language tutor, but that is later.
at the time of the family visit, my father pretends that
he is not home. when the teacher's briefcased figure appears

on the street, he simply goes up to the attic, which
later i am unable to explain. my grandmother
welcomes the homeroom teacher, they converse cheerfully,
i listen, only if they direct a question or two my way do i
answer, awkwardly. my grandmother scolds my father
terribly for his childish behavior. i will actually
come to like the homeroom teacher, yet all the same
i later retain only a few memory-pictures of him. for instance,
once, in front of the house, he is in the midst of beekeeping. around
the hives there is a yellow, humming cloud, and he wears gloves
and a face-protecting mesh. he gives me a face-protector too, and
lifts up a honeycomb, shows it to me. it's the first time i see such a thing;
yet my grandfather is a beekeeper too, he just dies before i am born.
another time there will be some event. a carnival or something
like that, there will be baked treats, and two of my companions move
at once for the very last biscuit. finally they split it,
and the homeroom teacher asks who got the bottom part. i thought
you did, he tells one of the boys. at which the other one laughs
out loud. this one gets embarrassed. the other is a star pupil,
the agronomist's son, and later this gets him somewhere in life.
the first one's father is a peasant, he keeps cattle, once i go
to their house for milk, the son at the moment is packing manure
into the wheelbarrow, let's say he's a good student too, but after
eighth grade he goes to vocational high school. the last time i
exchange words with him, at a market in another town, he is selling
vegetables, so we might be thirty years old. a few years later i hear
that he commits suicide, he hangs himself. besides keeping bees,
the homeroom teacher is a photographer. the school later purchases

several cameras, maybe the pajtás brand, and we can take the machines

home for a few days to make pictures. i seek out old houses,

fences in the other part of town. forty years later,

when there is no longer anyone for me to visit, i find

the forged gate, the crumbling walls, which as a child i shoot, but

afterward they will not be immortalized, since after

the homeroom teacher develops the film, most of the squares

reveal just dim spots, and only a few pictures identify me

as the one who took the reel, but even on those, the street houses

look vague and motion-blurred. but i like the displays.

later i do not learn the technique, but as for the view,

i try to edit it. to the extent possible.

# Slap

he will be a gypsy boy, or maybe half-gypsy; but this matters
only because of a spontaneous phrase. otherwise he is the same
kind of sweatsuited devil as the rest of us. at that time only the
agronomist's son wears jeans, and we envy him for it, but
also get along well with him. we go to upper elementary school,
maybe sixth grade, and during recess we play soccer with pieces
of tile on the pavement, because that has become our custom
over the years, as it has become our parents' to scold us, along with
a slap in the face for emphasis, for kicking our shoes to shreds.
if we do not play soccer, there's always something else to do.
say, talking about the previous night's films. i can't add to those
discussions, though, because we won't have a tv, i beg for one
in vain. my mother is willing to have one, but my father
digs his heels in: the radio's enough of a liar! but he still listens
to the news, and he pieces it together. sometimes he brings his ear
up close to the little box, when radio free europe is crackling or
the voice floats behind the rattling. so i don't know the series
in which the kuruc heroes defeat the half-witted, faint-hearted labanc
again and again, or partisans sacrifice their lives for us, so later,
when imaginary bullets fire from our fingers in the schoolyard,
in my soul i watch the whole thing from a step behind.
long live hitler! the half-gypsy *or maybe gypsy-all-the-way*
yells at one point, and fires furiously at his red-army classmates,
until our physics teacher arriving on the scene gives him a huge

slap in the face. the picture freezes. we stand there, a confused,
scared group of statues, and we hear, my little boy, hitler would
have sent you to the gas chamber along with the jews! in fact
you wouldn't even have been born! and so the game is over
for that recess, and flocking together we try to figure out
what that wouldntevenhavebeenborn could mean.

# Penknife

the glue of helplessness, the humbling defenselessness
is all that will remain of the story forty years later:
i head home from school, on some afternoon bending
toward evening, in any old time of year, a teenager.
my schoolbag is on my shoulder; in my mind, the future
flashes its splendid pictures: i will be a sheriff or the like,
and i will fight for order, for truth, for blond love with its
flowing locks, and will scratch my way out of danger. i then
head homeward, the sidewalk will be wet, the rain
falls in droplets from the fish-gray sky, i make my way
home slowly. it is all the same to me if i am soaked
by the time i arrive. the boys waiting for me do not care
about the rain either. around the bend, to the left, there will be
a poplar forest, to the right a wire fence, then a green
picket one, and where it ends, an alcove, about a meter long.
the house was built farther back than the fence, and this nook
is one heck of a hiding place. here we will scare each other
again and again: one of us runs ahead, as though hurrying,
then slips into the fence's crevice: bah or kaboom!
suddenly i am standing there in the corner, and three or four
boys surround and grab me, and they point a penknife
straight at my belly, and later i will not know for sure
what they wanted, if anything, or if they were just
trying to give me a good scare. they achieve the latter,

but as for the knife-wielder: he is a kid from next door,

his mother always spreads grease or jam on bread

for me, and my mother does the same for the boy.

at one point their dog will bite my leg, an enormous

white kuvasz sheepdog, but i am not badly hurt,

just pinched, barely a drop of blood will come out

of the wound, instead the tooth marks will be visible.

the boy is a year older than me, later i do not remember

the others, just him. and later we get along well.

we forget the knife incident, or else do not talk about it,

but my memory preserves it, and even forty years later

i can clearly see, if i shut my eyes, how under the fish-gray

sky, he pushes the fish-gray blade toward my stomach,

and the rain comes down, and then it stops. and i cannot know

how long the penknife idea lived in him, nor can i ask him

down the road, since the neighbors' son dies young,

somewhere in his thirties. i hear the news of his death

from my mother, on one of my visits. nonetheless

the whole thing is so unlikely that i do not believe it.

all the same, after the penknife adventure, my grandmother,

seeing my agitation, will ask me what's the matter. i will

not tell her what happened, but it is possible that i blurt

it out despite myself, and my grandmother has no choice

but to rush over to the neighbors and chide the mom

for not giving the little numskull a better upbringing.

since the action can unfold in various ways, the sequel,

too, has varied possibilities. and even when a single event

is chosen, it opens up into countless consequences.

certain possibilities close themselves off at last — yet,

if i forget a story, and only the glue of helplessness,

of humbling defenselessness remains, i can still

replay it again and again, always in a different way,

like the sheriff's moment of justice, or like blondness

fulfilled. i can rewrite my memories, but when i do,

the truth that then accompanies me to this poem,

does it stay the same?

# Pioneer

above is the egg-yellow sun, the sky is colorless, the air
an empty medium. no sounds land anywhere. there won't
even be sounds. a mute dream: we march in formation
in the schoolyard, and the female squad leader shouts. nothing
satisfies her. yet satisfaction will come (later she might even
get married). let the song be about april fourth or pioneer
induction day! in dark blue pants and white shirts we
bask in the sterile light of recollection, and i only
regret that my shirt has no shoulder-strap or buttoned
chest-pocket. i would really like the kind that timur
wears in the movie. i won't like my pioneer neckerchief
either, because it is made of canvas, while everyone else's
is silken, and the light glitters differently on theirs. it glitters
on theirs. my parents won't buy that kind, because if, say,
the canvas cost seventeen forints, the silk would cost twenty-three.
the difference is the price of two kilos of brown bread or three
bags of lemon drops. but we are saving up. we want to buy
a house so that we won't have to live with my grandmother. later
i too will have a silk neckerchief, but then i will already be
grown up: from teacher training i go to my old school for
summer practice, and at the camp, the loud teacher of my
tender age wakes me up in the morning with pálinka. she fills
a water cup with it, like misi nyilas's gym teacher, then sloshes
the cup again halfway. at that camp the teachers drink a heck

of a lot. i drink too: the candidate. at that camp there will be
beautiful teenage girls. i try not to get lost gazing at them. i don't
always succeed. at that camp the educators who drink their liquor
mostly straight up tell jokes and stories until dawn, but from
that camp i later remember just one concrete sentence
(a street gypsy says to his companions):
let there be a guitar in your depths, let cancer pluck it to death!
when i write this later, i think about how
there will surely be those who read for specific references,
and they will scold me for revealing that while the teachers
are partying until dawn, the teenage boys steal into the
teenage girls' cabins. but it's possible that i am just
inventing all of this, because pioneer camps are generally
like this. and non-pioneer camps too. and when it comes to reading,
almost everyone reads for references (especially if
they know the author), except maybe a few literati,
who have gathered up enough discipline not to let themselves
simplistically refer a complex of symbols to reality. maybe they are right,
because in the end, who could know, even from this poem,
what it is like to march out in pioneer uniform in nineteen seventy-three
or four, what it is like to feel or think anything whatsoever
on the concrete-paved schoolyard in that muted dream, whose silence,
due not to anxiety but to emptiness, becomes unbearably, irreversibly whole,
so that forty years later, even i don't know what it is like.

# Confession

i will have to go to religion classes when i am ten or
a little older, or maybe not that old. my mother says:
you are a big boy now, and she drags me to mass on sunday
mornings, whereas earlier she didn't go. she just starts
going because of me, to torture me. later i realize
all this hullabaloo is because of confirmation, of course
i don't know what confirmation is either. my mother
would explain, but i am not interested. it will be summer,
the sun shines yellowly, the melons ripen, and i go
to the cold church among children i don't know, to listen
to the things the old priest recounts, but i would rather hide
under the bed. my mother, when she finds me, whacks
me out with a broom, but nonetheless it is not easy to send
me to religion classes, a hearty spanking is required, and
it is not as if i had ideological reservations, i simply
would rather play at the end of the yard or out on the street
with the kids from next door. but there's nothing to be done
if this is the will of god, who watches everybody's every
moment, and when he sees an action that he doesn't like,
or even one he does, he writes it up in his big book, and
demands an account; there will be no evading
the thousand-eyed, thousand-handed prison guard.
in the chilly church the priest explains, but no one

pays attention, at most just once in a while, for example
when he shows us pictures in some huge, carcass-heavy book.
in one of them, two men in strange, scant clothes carry
enormous bunches of grapes on poles over their shoulders,
bunches as big as they are, and each grape as big
as the men's heads, they are that big. you could play
ball with them, but biting into them is hard. so, that
will be canaan! the geography teacher promises it too,
she just calls it communism, and when we ask when
it will come, she thinks it over a little, then replies:
two hundred years from now. all the same i will not
be able to get that grape picture out of my head. truly
that's the only thing that remains from religion classes,
and later, when i grow up, i leaf through illustrated bibles
in antique bookstores, hoping to come upon that painting,
supposing the whole thing could start over again—give me a
definite time, and i will twist my life out of place! i will
also remember the colorful glass panes of the church windows,
i love to look at them during dull masses, where i sit between
many old women, next to my mother, who is still young.
and i stare at the stations, the frescoes, the gray-bearded
old man on the ceiling. i think he is god. i will fear him, but
i look at him nonetheless. and the wafer, which the priest
drops onto my tongue, and i bite. my mother says i mustn't,
since that is jesus's body. my guilt strikes, i get scared that
i have chewed the baby jesus, who brings the christmas tree
and a sweater, thermal socks, and sometimes a book.

as a sinner i can go confess one morning. i kneel before
the priest, there is some wooden lattice between us, and
i don't know what i am supposed to do, since i am not
listening when he explains. i am tongue-tied, and he says:
repeat after me! and i mutter after him: i have not honored
my father, my mother, i have killed, i have committed
adultery, i have stolen, i have lied, i have coveted my
neighbor's wife. i say the words, and i do not understand
the words, i kneel before uncle priest, i don't understand
uncle priest, or god either. or the world. what is a
neighbor, and what does it mean to covet his wife? and if
the priest had killed someone, would he still say what he
is saying? and why do i repeat after him, when i have not
killed, at least nothing more than bugs, mosquitoes,
flies, but we don't kill them, we swat them. and what does
it mean to commit adultery? that i sometimes play with myself,
or that in the outhouse in the yard, i look through the deck
of cards i stole from my father, which he borrowed from someone,
and which has young women displaying themselves in panties
and bras? i mutter the words, the priest inflicts the penance
and says goodbye, but i would like to go back to him
to confess: uncle priest, i lied: i haven't killed anyone yet,
and i don't even understand why i said it. of course i do not
go back, but if years later i see the priest, it occurs to me
that i should say: i am not a murderer, i just lied,
and that isn't such a great sin anyway. or if indeed it is,
the thousand-eyed one knows everything already, and

supposedly sees into our thoughts as well, like a secret
agent or an informer—which means that i will also have
to exercise caution with what i think forty years later
about heavenly and earthly canaan.

# Schoolyard

i will be a tall, strong child. one of the strongest
in the class. if we include the b-class, even then
i end up with just three or four tough opponents. but
we don't fight much, although at the sandbox (which
of course is not a sandbox, but rather a wide sand trough
built under the schoolyard's climbing ropes and rings) we wrestle
sometimes. the yard attendant does not look that way. the ropes
are actually held up by thick iron pipes painted light blue, the sand
will always be dry in my memory, because the sun will shine
continually, and the shadows will be short, and we wait
for the bell to ring. or we don't wait for it, because we would like
recess to last forever. and that is not exactly correct.
rather, we wish no lesson would start up. we loiter in groups and alone
around the climbing-ropes. boys and girls together, but separated
all the same. sometimes the girls' panties flash in the sunlight.
because the sun will always be shining. even when it isn't,
then too. if instead it's raining or snowing, they don't let us
leave the corridor, lest we track in mud on our shoes. later
concrete covers the schoolyard almost everywhere, but when
i go there, i don't even know what kind it is. maybe cinder. or maybe
nothing. there will be two gates, so we can play soccer—true,
just at the end of gym class, as a reward. since there aren't
many balls around, we kick tile pieces into an ad-hoc gate by the
one-storied back building. that's where the manual workrooms are,

where we make small wooden things with jigsaws and the like, while
the girls learn knitting and cooking. when we play soccer
with pieces of tile, the teachers often write me up, since someone
excused from gym class should not be running around. i am excused
due to a misdiagnosis, even though i am a strong child.
but not a fighter. nonetheless we always find some pretext for
a little rascalry. we fight our way into groups, we form cliques, and
teasing thoughts sometimes lead to physical tests of strength:
jostling, a kick in the shin, a punch in the ribs, tussles, panting,
torn clothes. then peacemaking, dusting off clothes, or running away.
never serious. just once will it get a bit rough: at the yard outhouse,
where they have painted the wall at least a meter high with black
oil paint. we urinate on the oil while watching it splatter and the juice
drip yellow down a trough next to the wall. there the concrete will
always be wet, there will be scattered traces of urine; in short,
there will be three or four of us in the bathroom, and i will be just
going out, when a short, blond, chubby boy, one grade behind us, comes
along and suddenly, without a word, hits me in the face, so that my nose
begins to bleed. when i write this, i no longer remember
the reason, if there is one in the first place, just that
i don't hit him back. there's no ganging up, no fan alliances, and i
take out my crumpled handkerchief, which i always have on me, and
slink farther away. the story will not have a sequel, although i often
run into the boy in the schoolyard. at such times my stomach
initially tightens, then i get used to the fact that we have
a common, one-sided story. with no origin or
consequence. the boy will have a bunch of siblings, but
after school they will go home in opposite directions. they head

out to the poor part of town. of course we are poor too; they
are just more so. my parents call their kind: lumpen.
decades later, when i go back home to the village
where my childhood passes by, we run into each other
in company. i don't recognize him, i just notice his last name
when they introduce us. i say my own, to which he replies
that he recognizes me because i look like my father.
we have a friendly chat, i ask him how old he is, to find out
whether i might not be speaking with one of his brothers. no,
it's him! but does he remember that in the schoolyard
the sun is always shining, and that the girls' panties sometimes
flash from beneath their short skirts?

# Time Change

for some reason i am held after school. being held
means that as punishment i cannot go home after class,
because, let's say, i don't do my lesson, i answer
badly, i don't pay attention or i misbehave, the teacher
notices, and after the lesson she puts a few of us
in a room: she gives an extra lesson, or we have to
do homework, or maybe write a sentence a hundred times,
consisting of maybe a promise or a moral. i rarely am held
after school, maybe just once, when the geography teacher,
who teaches that in two hundred years communism will
replace socialism, doesn't let me go home when classes
are over. later i no longer remember what my
omission or commission was. i don't remember staying
after school either, just the moment when i am
told, and later heading home and wondering what
to say about why i was late. that is, according to
my parents, being held after school is an unpardonable
offense, proof that i didn't do something or did it
poorly. uneasily i head home, i am about
twelve years old, i open the gate, the weather is nice,
my grandmother and father are busying themselves
in the foyer, and they are acting so naturally, as if
i weren't a whole hour late. i peer into the kitchen.
i see that the alarm clock says one-thirty, but

it is actually two-thirty. i relax: it is wrong, so

my parents won't notice my lateness. this means

i won't be suspected either, when my father asks

what time it is, and i lie, telling him what the

clock hands say. my father asks this and that:

whether everything was okay at school and on

the way home. with a sense of relief, i nod, fine,

of course. everything is fine. but when he asks

whether i stayed after school, it is time for me

to arouse his suspicions by saying that one

of my classmates from the neighboring street

blurted something out. and so the world collapses

for an afternoon or a week. maybe my father

gives me a beating, maybe i just get to hear

the lecture: it isn't enough that i am held after school,

i lie too, and i had a chance to admit to it, since

he asked me about it. yes, but in the meantime

he also gave me the possibility, the temptation, to get

away with it, since the only time the clock is wrong

is when my father turns the hands back, to set

a trap for his child who thinks then—and later too,

since this story often comes to mind in his

adulthood—anyway, who thinks: that turning

the clock hands back is no smaller a lie than any

human relation.

# Fool

he comes with aluminum jugs to the well. for years, decades
he has been carrying his drinks, in winter, summer, as long
as water is not conveyed into their yard. but at this time they
already live indoors, they move from the farm at the village's edge
onto our street. he always wears a workers' suit, dark blue,
new or worn gray and stained. on his head there is a tilted
beret; his outfit includes a cigarette stump eternally sticking
out from under his nicotine-yellow hitler mustache. a tall,
handsome, strong young man, always smiling: the neighborhood
fool. he drags the jugs along at an easy pace, stares
monotonously at the ground in front of him, or carries the water
with his mouth drawn into a smile. we kids often start up conversation
with him; he puts down the jug, and we chat. we don't dare mock him,
since then he raises his huge palm, and we know that he
is very strong. he says, let's hand-wrestle, and then
the bigger boys try in vain. he always wins, and the one
whose hand he cracks straightens out his crippled fingers
in astonishment. otherwise a pious soul. it is possible to
talk with him about holy things. about women, about love
for example. if a girl or young woman goes by us, he gives
his tilted head a better twist, or else he smiles and,
rotating his whole body toward the women, ogles them.
he makes mischievous comments. we have a good snigger
at these, and egg him on to even wilder indecency with

the women and with the subject of love in general.
he likes to chat with us, and we often beat our boredom
with him, until his foolishness bores us too. then he picks
up his jugs and takes them to the nearby farm. he always
dresses for the season: sandals, shoes, rubber boots.
but he never wears gloves. he says he isn't cold,
and we believe him, although his rough, big hands get
red in winter, and i picture his fingernails as blue, when
i write this. after they move from the farm, he doesn't have
to carry water any more, they just send him to the store for bread,
cigarettes, pálinka. his teeth get yellow from nicotine,
his smile will be yellower too; his face, cobwebbed with the fine
wrinkles of the years. we speak less and less, but still
talk now and then. i exchange theories with the fool in
a sober world. later on he remains alone in the house,
his immediate family dies. relatives visit him,
bring him cooked food on weekends, and during the week
he carries home lunch in a lunchbox from the nursery school
kitchen. you can ask him: what's for lunch? and if he
has eaten it, how did it taste? later i move away, and
i will not learn a thing about him. when i write this,
i do not remember the news of his death, but i think
he has long stopped bringing home cigarettes and food
for himself, and others for him.

# Madeleine

when i go running by the meat factory, i get a whiff
of some familiar scent. of the old slaughterhouse, where
my father and mother both work for a time. as a child
i will detest that smell, which is not the dung-stench
of pigs awaiting their execution, nor the smell of blood
draining away, nor of deflectors, trucks, an intestine plant,
nor the bitter smell of distant smoke-houses or the cold scent
of meat refrigeration rooms, nor of sausage mountains, but:
the smell of fat. and not of the tubs of lard at home, where
the pork side pieces lie flat, nor of boiling fat, greaves
of fresh roast, but of cold grease, the vapor of piglets
slit open, the chopping rooms' pure tile, the peculiar
fluids spreading over the metal table, the meat and bacon
shreds slapped by the hose's jet, the inexpungible stench
of dressing rooms, where the hybrid odor eats its way
into everything: the gowns, the street clothes hanging
in the tin wardrobe, the rubber boots all over the place,
the joints between the wall-tiles, the concrete,
the workers' skin, the embraces they bring home.
i will detest that smell, but the slaughterhouse
in its complex entirety i will love nonetheless. it will be
the world of grownups: of loud words, coarse jokes,
lively gossip. at home i soak up slaughterhouse stories,
who said what to whom, what happened to whom.

my mother works in the intestine plant. for years on end,
eight hours a day, she cleans pig intestines. if at school
they ask me about my parents' professions, i reluctantly
say meat processing plant, but about their actual work
i do not utter a word. i stammer that i don't know, since
i would rather be deemed a dunce than tell the truth.
my father will be a janitor, they give him a service cap,
but he won't wear it. at home i will play police with it.
still i will be ashamed of my father's work, because
he is ashamed too. but after his disability leave, he can
be glad he has a job. it is not easy work, to be sure.
they constantly have him doing something: weighing,
smoking, cleaning the yard, doing the janitorial tasks.
he works countless night shifts, and often does not
even come home on weekends. sometimes i bring
him dinner. on such occasions he detains me,
keeps showing me the factory, what is what,
the smoke room larders, the forest of sausages and
salamis hanging from rods on high-running rails,
the packed rows of thick hams, and down below,
the red-white sawdust sends up its smoke.
the flammable material runs in strips, you have to feed
the live coal with a shovel, sometimes i help sprinkle
the fragrant sawdust. at such times i try hard
not to inhale the smoke. my father tries too, but
it ends up in his lungs again and again, and when
the cancer takes off inside him and multiplies,
i will believe his illness was caused by some

work injury. later, several decades after childhood,

i take regular runs by another tall meat factory

and get a familiar whiff of that old smell. i will be

married, and my wife, who sometimes runs with me,

will grimace on account of the stench, which to me is so

familiar that it verges on the pleasant—just like

a madeleine.

# American Chocolate

i will not have an american great-uncle, or a great-uncle at all,
but one of my father's friends is a dissident in fifty-six. first
he tries to make it in italy, then after after the divorce
starts a new life in the new world. he rarely exchanges postcards
with my father, but through correspondence with his parents
they keep track of each others' basics: marriage, the birth
of children. when he visits hungary, he and his daughter
look us up. he brings presents: american chocolate,
nail-clippers, a good, large cap. trifles that nonetheless seem
important to me. the nail-clippers will be a minor redemption, since
we used to cut our nails with a tailor's scissors. my mother, grandmother,
later i. the blades leave a rough surface behind, it bothers me
that my nails keep getting stuck in my clothes and i live in terrible
awkwardness. the cap will be the kind that mcmurphy wears
in one flew over the cuckoo's nest, and later it becomes known
as an attribute of the writer tandori. my own cap is green,
let's say medium-green! my mother does not force me
to wear it, and i would be ashamed of its color (lead-heavy
little town, lead-heavy years), so it lies low for a long time
in some cabinet or other. maybe i wear it for a few days
when i have lost my usual cap and we have not yet bought
a new one. later as an adult i come to love it, because it has
a color like no other. by now i can be recognized in it
from far away. but then my wife starts to get embarrassed.

maybe by the color, but also because i wear it to tatters. at the top
the material starts to decompose, and no one will be able to crochet
it back into commission, so once again the poor cap ends up
at the bottom of the cabinet. when my father's friend visits
us with his half-italian daughter, just a couple of years younger
than me, it will be summer: skirt-bouncy, braid-swinging.
the uncle-friend asks me something, i mutter a reply, to which
the thin-faced, maybe bespectacled american engineer asks
me again, and then i answer more loudly. we sit
on the shady veranda or in the chilly room, and i listen to
the adult discussion, which is probably exactly the sort that happens
when two people who once knew each other well meet twenty
years later. i would gladly play with the girl, but we do not
understand each other's language, and just sit politely as long as
the visit lasts. still i think back on her sometimes. she will be
my faraway italian love. when i write this later, i imagine
what kind of donna she might be. if i were to meet her, of course
we would not recognize each other, since i don't even remember
her childhood face. just that she is beautiful: bella.
or maybe even not so much. a little bit stocky. a little bit
whatever. in the end we are just bound together by our fathers'
little bit of shared youth. that is, by nothing. when i write this,
my father will be long dead, and i will no longer remember the taste
of the american chocolate.

# Construction

the young couple buys the lot in the row of gable-roofed
houses, and construction begins. the man will be tall, thin,
bespectacled (at that time almost all glasses have thick
rims), and walks around in gym shorts. his wife is a blond,
slightly plump, but still shapely young woman, the eternal
wearer of a black bikini. when stolid men bicycle
past their entrance, they unconsciously turn toward it,
their eyes seeking out the young woman bending over.
for they constantly work there, they have been building
their house for years, the two of them. after work they rest
their bikes against the wire fence and dig a foundation,
mix concrete, put up a wall made of a new kind of
cube brick, and the windows that will be in the wall,
and install the tent roof's wood frame together, and put up
the gray slate together, everything they make together: a house,
three children. later i remember just the summers, the plain
summer twilights, when i go to the well for water, and
while the thin stream trickles into the cans, i look at them,
the ones who will have a beautiful house, with a tent roof,
modern, large-windowed. and there will be electricity
already on the plot, because if it gets dark, they will keep
on working by the light of the bare bulb. even on weekends.
there will be a sand-hill in the yard, yellow in the rain,
colorless in dry weather, and until it ends up in the mortar,

the yellow-haired children play in it: in panties, shorts.
it will be summer, the ditch grass burns down, the naked
skin burns, then turns brown. it's possible that they build
for just a year or two, but later on the era of my childhood's
passing seems endless, and the houseless couple's house
gets built, although for a long time it stays unfinished:
they don't paint it, they don't sand the rough plaster, and
the yard, too, is a mess for years, as if an imaginary sign
remained outside, stating that it is a construction lot
(since the intention remains true even when the money
runs out). for a long time their windows will have no curtains,
just the tv's blue color will drip out into the night puddles,
and the blond children grow up, and later i will have no idea
how many of them are boys or girls. nor will i know what
has become of the couple, and who will live forty years later
in the cube house that they built. whether they bring up
the children together? or break up? onto the great summers
come winter, cold.

# Hospital

the gypsy girl will have short hair, her body is pretty and arched,
but her eyes blunt and lightless, as she looks through the glass
separating the hospital rooms—and one night, when
my heart beats like crazy, they turn on the neon lights
in the neighboring room: nurses and doctors rush,
outside the houses *swim in the moonlight,* as do *the gardens,* and
the dogs howl, but i will not hear them, because my attention
is elsewhere, because the girl's roaring sore throat mutes everything else.
she tosses on the bed, where her naked body is bound,
and they cover her with a sheet, which she constantly shifts off of her,
and the infusion drips into her, and my heart fills up with squeaking
fear, and i sleep at dawn, when the squeaking loses its voice.
and the next day the gypsy girl just lies motionless on the bed,
she no longer shouts, she is *silent with stubborn lips,* and in
her white sheet she will be *just like a* broken-eyed black *angel.* and when
i write this poem, i no longer remember how many days she lies
there, tied to the infusion, with emptied eyes, just that
*one morning i stare in alarm* at her empty bed, and
i guess, by myself or with my roommates, that she either
was moved to another department or died. i will be fourteen
at the time, i stay two months in the hospital, and out of self-diligence
i take my own pulse many times a day. they say i am on bedrest.
i can't get up either, except to go to the bathroom, and then
the doctors make their rounds, the women doctors deliberate

at the end of the bed, and the head doctor asks me once, when
examining a girl smaller than me in the neighboring bed, to look
away, and i do it blushing, while my heart pounds loudly: *what
can it be—my god—what?* confessions of felix krull, let that be
the title of the book i read then. decades later i will no longer
remember anything from it, just the title, and that it is fairly
thick. thomas mann wrote it, whose magic mountain i do not read,
a fact that later gives me shame. i lie then on the hospital bed,
the book in my hands, and stare above it at the lazy movements
of the young nurse on night shift, how she arranges the thermometers
and syringes on a tray. and time slows down, stops.
i need to read that novel over again, for the chance to get swept
up into its plot and vortex. and when, drowned, i would look up from
its midst, i would see darkness lurking in the ninth-floor hospital
window, but would stare instead at the beautiful night nurse.
and then suddenly the silence would crack, and time
would start up again, and i would go along with it, still believing,
at the time, that i had a say in the destination.

# Death Jump

for a long time we will not have a tv, but i wish badly for one.
as a child i will not be able to comprehend how, if almost everyone
on the street has one, even those poorer than ourselves, why
we can't have one too. for example when they broadcast the series
called the captain of the outlaws, the next day at school i can't
follow the warrior games. of course if they ask, i say that i saw
the film too, but i just watch the enthusiasms from a distance: i can't
comment with any authority on the kuruc-labanc question.
when thorn castle is on television, this time i read the novel, but it
is not required, and the teacher asks who saw the film. so as not
to stick out, i raise my hand, and the teacher calls precisely on me,
and asks who that matula character is. but i am still at the beginning
of the story and will not know. of course the class bursts out
laughing, the teacher however wonders how the hell i don't know.
how can i be so stupid? and so i think i am unlucky, since she
happened to grill me just now, later i suspect she knows that we
have no tv and calls on me for that very reason. the transparent
shame of glassy silence stays familiar later on too: in high school,
in our homeroom class, we have to list the names of tv announcers,
demonstrating our interest in current politics, so that we can watch
the news properly, since this is required. but i would rather stand
in the bell jar again than admit that we don't have a tv and that's
why i can't list the announcers' fucking names. and yet once
in a while i go with my father to the neighbors behind our house

to watch tv. several faces from it will be familiar: the pipe-smoking
news commentator, the delta science series presenter, at some point
they will broadcast some italian circus series too. the title will be salto
mortale, and for months afterward i will want to be a circus artist:
i practice somersaults, trapeze jumps on the straw bales, the bundles
of cornstalks, the mulberry branches. my classmates watch that
series too, they talk about it during recess, act it out as much as
possible. but i do none of this with them, or with others either,
never, ever.

# Piano

forty years later the picture will not be clear. i will
not remember whether it is fall or winter, just that it gets
dark early, and through the culture house window,
opened just a crack, the sound of a piano tumbles
onto the street. maybe it is fall after all. late autumn.
or maybe the tiny room is overheated, where my classmate
hammers away at the pianino. a moment later, from
the dark outdoors, i see a hobbling old teacher give him
a clap on the ear. all the same i envy him for being able
to play. i will hate the teacher. from the sidewalk i gaze
through the window, inhaling the scent, like rimbaud's urchins,
a scent of that world which is visible only from afar,
because we live at the edge of the village, where
there is no paved road yet, just a sidewalk, which gets mud
dragged onto it by horsecarts and tractors crossing
the street on rainy days, and later we have to scrape it
from our boots. when i gaze through the slightly opened
window, that is, in early adolescence, the street lamps
barely light up the surroundings. there will be few vehicles,
but instead old women in work trousers, men in fur caps
will go by on foot. or else they will haul bags of powdered
feed for the porkers. there will also be one who ties
two sacks to his bicycle crossbar. not far away, the window
of the flat-roofed department store will cast light

onto the street. the building has only just opened, and
compared to the former one it abounds in inventory,
so we will not have to take the train to the nearest city
whenever we want to buy shoes. people will heat their homes
with coal, pressure will hold down the smoke, but we
will not have heard about smog yet, i will not know that
it is unhealthy; besides, i will acutely enjoy the bitterish,
stifling smell. later i will not remember what i was seeking
that evening, in front of the culture house. maybe my parents
sent me to the abc grocery? but the clearest memory i have
is of the happy yet bitterish moment when from below
my classmate's hand the sounds of music tumble out
onto the smoke-scented, pre-christmas street, where
people come and go, greet and speak to each other, and i
think of one thing alone: if only i could sit at the piano,
coax sounds from instruments. guitar would be good too.
or harmonica. but i can't even sing. i just like to. everyone
laughs at me because i have no ear for music. so they say.
my mother laughs, my grandmother sighs, my music teacher
gives a wave of the hand, later my children laugh at me too.
so what makes it happy, then, that bittersweet moment
in front of the culture house? maybe that i still imagine
a future that will not come to pass. but forty years later
the lack of it will no longer trouble me – slowly
i get used to myself.

# Indifferent

in elementary school he is in the parallel class. he will be
a quiet, soft-spoken, thin, swarthy boy. he combs his hair upwards,
just as i do at that time. nothing about him stands out.
after eighth grade he becomes a business apprentice, that is,
in vocational school he learns how to be a shop assistant
and has to go for practice. they assign him to the little
store on the corner, i hurry by every day on my way to
the high school, and sometimes we meet. we greet
each other but don't talk for long. both of us will be
reticent little chaps. or maybe sometimes he is the one
who speaks up, who asks something indifferent: what's up,
how's it going? some plain thing that can be answered
in banalities. later i no longer remember whether
we ever meet inside the store, just as from that general
time frame i can't recall a single occasion from when
we still were in elementary school. just this remains,
the way he sweeps the sidewalk in front of the store
with a broom in the mornings, i walk over it
umpteen times. he will have a huge, blue jacket on,
not the kind that we have to wear in high school,
but longer, reaching all the way to his knees,
and maybe one size larger than necessary.
he will be a skinny boy, sixteen years old. it's as if
i could remember his voice when he says hello,

and asks something unanswerably indifferent,

and sweeps, and sweeps, and once later does not sweep,

and then they say that he is sick but afterwards

he sweeps again (just a little paler, just a little

skinnier, more speechless), so that at last

he may never sweep again, since he has something

incurable. blood cancer, i remember later,

that's what they call it. after he gets sick, maybe

we no longer exchange even a pair of indifferent words.

he doesn't take the initiative, and neither do i. but when

they post his obituary in the window of the funeral home,

i go there many times and read: he lived seventeen years,

and i add in my thoughts: he can never know what it is like

to be in love, at most he knows the unrequited, hopeless kind.

at that time i won't know more about love either, nor will i

know any more than he does about death. almost nothing.

let's say he will know much more about death than i.

or to put it more precisely: at seventeen he will know more.

since, after all, who can know the future?

# Meadow

it could be winter: patches of snow on the frozen ground, and creeping under
the gardens, the smell of smoke, which i love so much! it could be spring too:
brave with lenten winds. or autumn: depression pregnant with rainclouds. but
let it instead be summer again! gentle summer. or any afternoon regardless
of season: the clouds uncover and cover the sun: all right, let it be undershirt
summer after all! let the footpath below the gardens lead to the train tracks,
to the forbidden area, where i never go with the band of kids, just sometimes
with my father, in the sultry heat after the rain, to pick mushrooms in big baskets
next to the cow droppings, because that is where the herd path will be.
or let there be snow! not the kind with slow, large flakes, but rather like grains
in the rough wind. an early november snowfall that sends you dashing home
into the homelike aroma of goose roast, and watch dinner cooking in the huge
cast-iron pan. let it be real winter! with freezing feet in soaked boots, but to slide
to the point of numbness, to scratch the tractor tracks' frozen puddles with your
iron heel-plates, then in a commonplace spring season to absorb the heavy
smell of the naked earth, where the sowing turns green between the puddles,
and the wind sweeps the possibilities of faraway lands, and carries them along
mercilessly. the cheap train hauled by the steam engine is later replaced
by a red diesel train; sometimes we ride it to my grandparents in the next
village, and sometimes elsewhere too, but mostly i just hear the sound below
the gardens, the heavy, dragged-out whistle, and if wind comes from it, it brings
the sound of clicking wheels along, and the seasons revolve around the fungal
meadow. all the same, time goes in one direction. and the one who has been
traveling with it for a while can  at most look back.

# Superstitions

where is the origin? does the number line run forward or backward? and
where will i be? where will i stand on that page, onto which an unknown
hand draws childhood—for me? a childhood you cannot grow
up out of. i count the sidewalk squares on the way to school; i always
walk on the line. or between the lines. i am superstitious, but later i
no longer remember what means what. i get tangled in square meshes.
i will know the numbers, but i do not care for them. the black tomcat
will chew the heads of his own kittens, their eyes still unopened, in
the empty beehive. of the four frail whining voices first three, then two,
then later one remains, and then green bottleflies start to buzz over
the silent mucous membrane. cats have seven lives. or nine.
hell and heaven! the extended anxiety of old women in headscarves
who speak of witches as though their existence were certain.
my mother nods, and there is no one to contradict them. i have to
invent my own fallacies. if i see a chimney sweep, i take hold of my
lowest button, and i squeeze it until i meet three people
wearing glasses. or until my fingers start to hurt. i must not
let luck slip away. in the flat pan on the cooking range, the milk
suddenly begins to rise. take care, my father says in the morning,
it's friday, and moreover the thirteenth. besides milk i get
a badly cut, thick slice of bread. mornings without appetite.
the milk is white, blood is red. the blood of a bald-necked black
pullet foams in a little bowl. my father plays the lottery. dozens
of tickets, magic numbers. he never wins. in fact he is convinced

that they cheat, but he plays nonetheless. he asks me to say numbers
between one and ninety. once a four slips in. then they pay the lowest
prize in the history of the lottery, and my father desperately keeps on
amoeba-ing his five numbers, never choosing the number thirteen, and never
winning either. how could the poor man win, when they have the drawings
on fridays. he will be addicted to the ninety grid squares, but
his superstition will not whisk my childhood out of poverty. nor
can i whisk myself out of my childhood. however, my lucky
number will be thirteen. or not, since combined with
friday it remains the same as any other. later on i sometimes still
count the sidewalk squares and my steps, but if i see a black cat,
i will never again turn back from anywhere.

# Passageways to God

there will be my mother's church, my father's too,
my grandmother's. i am christened in the first of these,
the catholic one, where i must go for bible school and mass. but
my father's line is protestant, and my grandmother often
derides my mother's family as papist. and thus me too. grandmother
does not like papists. it hurts that at such times she does not
like me either. of course it's my mother's family, first and foremost,
that she dislikes. strictly speaking this is not dislike, but rather
contempt. the artisan's wife looks down on peasants and extends
her prejudice to religion. in practice it looks as if she views
catholics as a stupid, naive rabble who worship icons. capable
of eating rabbits, for instance. and a rabbit's flesh is the same
as a cat's. she says this because my mother's family
raises rabbits. of course, how and from what source could
my poor grandmother know what rabbit meat is like? still,
my entire life long, she discourages me from eating rabbits.
now and then my mother and i go to the catholic church, and
my father sometimes joins us. but rarely do my father and i
go to the protestant church, which my mother never attends.
even my father goes just twice a year, at new year's and easter.
but not always on new years. since it shaves away the time.
i don't know whether he skips services on purpose.
or whether he believes in god. but if he does, i somehow
don't believe it. the catholic church is not small and

not big. quite average. it will have a church smell. or else
a smell of old women. i sit at mass and try to put together
the story of the man with the crown of thorns. i keep looking
at the colored windows, not the saints painted on them, just
the play of colors, the way the glass lets the light through. if
there is a heaven after all, this could be the entry to some
other world. the protestant church will be different. two-towered,
with two lofts. white room, vast walls. once, by way of the spiral
staircase covered with pigeon droppings, my father takes me up
to a tower. we step out to the fire-watch balcony, in front
of the towers, to the narrow plank, but i don't dare lean against
the thin iron railings, i don't dare rest my elbows on them,
since i fear that they will come loose from the wall. we
will be thirty meters above the city. in horror i take in
the cluster of houses, the streets' geometry, people bicycling
on the highways into space, to be absorbed somewhere
as dots in the bluish regions of the color field. i see
what god more or less might see as well. and what i don't see, that
is only because it is inside the houses, or shielded by trees, rows
of acacia. i am afraid of the depths but cannot get my fill of
the view. later it occurs to me that god must be equally anxious when
he looks down at the earth.

# Litterfall

the poplar trees will turn yellow then, when
one night a sudden chill descends on them, and not
leaf by leaf, like the happy trees, but from one day
to the next the entire forest turns yellow, and in the
weakening day the senile leaves lose their hold on
the branches. at the end of their hesitant descent, they
fatten the fresh layer of litterfall, so that then, having dried
into brown, the dead leaf-sheets may rattle under my feet;
they may break, crumble, their tiny pieces sneak their way
into shoes, penetrate their way through socks,
become nuisances, and i may walk through dry litterfall
up to my ankles; or if it is raining, the many fallen leaves'
color may brighten, deepen, become entirely dark, slimy,
slippery, soak my footwear as i wander in the forest,
the litterfall may hide the smaller holes in the ground,
where the water lies, and i may splash in them, since
it won't matter anyway, who cares if it prickles or soaks,
i will be alone, like god or those few bird-creatures
in the trees who turn their heads but otherwise stay rigid;
and let me be even more alone, even more
foreign, and if behind the clouds the sun flows into
the late afternoon, then the light may filter through the trees
as if it made sense, as if it were still possible; and if
the waters dry up, and when i stick a stick into the litterfall,

i may see last year's leaf layer, the one before last year,

the thick, fat litterfall may show its year-rings like

an archaeological find, but below it the earth may stay

slimy, wet and cold, with disgusting crawlers, worms,

earthworms, cocooned lives, deaths, if it is summer,

since then the new greenery will cover the ground

with shadow, there will be no telling where the litterfall's

bottom is, and at which point rotten leaves become fertile soil;

and i walk alone through the forest, and the litterfall

prickles and soaks, and i count the sun's rotations sweeping

the sky, and the birds, frightened, fly far away. and only

god huddles at the top of some poplar or other.

# Translator's Afterword

IN THE AUTUMN OF 2018, during my second year of teaching in Hungary, I came upon my colleague Gyula Jenei's poetry and immediately memorized one of the poems. That, in a sense, was the beginning of a project that I could not have foreseen. Many discoveries lay ahead; I soon found out that Jenei, as founder and editor-in-chief of the literary journal *Eső (Rain)*, brings some of Hungary's most interesting writers into print and to literary events. I discovered that his wife, Marianna Fekete, is a literary critic; her luminous essay on Béla Markó's haiku poems moved me to translate it, along with Jenei's poem "Standing Point," which opens this volume. More translations of Jenei's poetry followed; five were published in *Literary Matters*, and another in *The Massachusetts Review*. The three of us—Jenei, Fekete, and I—met from time to time and had long conversations: about the poems and their many allusions; about Hungarian literature; about education; about changes in Hungarian and U.S. American life over the decades; and much more. In October 2019, the three of us traveled to Dallas to give readings and lead discussions as the featured guests of the Dallas Institute of Education and Culture's Education Forum, hosted by the Institute's Cowan Center for Education. It was during this time that we met Will Evans, publisher of Deep Vellum, who brought up the possibility of a book.

The poems in this collection—the entirety of Jenei's 2018 collection, *Mindig más*, translated in sequence—constitute a unity. All involve a particular conception of time: the poet imagines himself forty years ago, as a young boy, looking around him and ahead into the future, which is the author's past. The poems have a gently prophetic feel: the things that they say will happen, actually did. At the same time, they play with the unreliable nature of memory: its uncertainties and gaps, its confusions and transpositions, its mixture of clarity and haze. All the while, each poem tells a story, or several; sometimes the story shifts midway and turns out to be about something else. Sometimes the narrator picks up on a detail and follows it to a surprising conclusion. Humor, melancholy, irony, self-questioning, and other stances alternate and mix.

The poems are written in free verse; they have the feel of short epics with relatively long lines and a discernible, though variable rhythm. The line breaks are important yet flexible; many of these poems in earlier versions had somewhat different line breaks, and the shift made a difference in the overall meaning. When deciding where to break the lines in the translations, I considered, first and foremost, the breaks in the original, along with syntax, rhythm, and subtle surprise. When ending each translated poem, I approximated the weight and twist of the ending in the original text.

Readers should have little difficulty understanding the poems in translation; the stories they tell, and the questions of time and memory surrounding them, are recognizable and in some ways universal. Yet some of the references require a brief explanation.

"Radio" refers to several radio programs and features of the 1960s and '70s, including Radio Free Europe (mentioned in the poem "Slap" as well) and the song "Kósza szél" ("Stray Wind") by Pál Szécsi. The latter has the following lyrics in the chorus (translated here): "Stray wind in the clouds' soft lap, / Board it with us, to another world fly. / Small boat on the sea of dreams, / Inside it sit a girl and I."

"Dread" begins with the mention of "revolutionary songs"; in the original, the phrase is "mozgalmi dallamok," which means, roughly, "workers' movement melodies," "revolutionary melodies," or something similar. This phrase evokes songs with a march-like beat and socialist patriotic content.

In "Uncle Doctor," the words in italics are quotations from Dezső Kosztolányi's poem by almost the same name (the only difference between the two titles is the definite article in the latter). In Hungary, "Uncle" and "Aunt" are often used as terms of respect—usually by children, when they speak or refer to a teacher, other professional, or friend of the family. Jenei's poem both evokes and diverges from Kosztolányi's; the reader will be able to discern the movement.

"Homeroom Teacher," likewise, evokes another poem through use of italics, albeit more briefly: Zoltán Somlyó's "Jajgató Felicián" ("Wailing Felicián"), about an eccentric, solitary, wailing man. In "Homeroom Teacher," by contrast, the eccentricity, solitude, and wailing, rather than collecting in one individual, spread all around the poem's environs: to the speaker's father, who hides in the attic when the homeroom teacher comes over for dinner; to the teacher himself, who absorbs himself in beekeeping; to one of the speaker's classmates, who later commits suicide; and to the speaker's photographs, which come out vague and motion-blurred.

Three poems, "Earth," "Slap," and "Death Jump," refer to the *kuruc*, a group of anti-Habsburg rebels led by Francis II Rákóczi in his War of Independence from 1703 to 1711. Their opponents, the *labanc* (mentioned in the latter two poems), were Hungarians and Austrians who sought to defend the House of Habsburg against the kuruc. The "kuruc-labanc question" refers not only to the historical issues, but to the ongoing tension between national independence and international dependence.

Like "Uncle Doctor," "Hospital" quotes from a Kosztolányi poem, this time "Azon az éjjel" ("That night"), in which the speaker tells of his grandfather's death. Here, in "Hospital," the speaker sees a Roma girl in a neighboring bed, struggling with illness, tossing and screaming, then silent the next morning, then gone—perhaps dead? Perhaps moved to a different part of the hospital?—and later, again, a new girl in a neighboring bed brings out his alarm. The italics indicate both Kosztolányi references and the speaker's own anxiety; death and illness never belong to one person alone. Yet the speaker, a child, does not yet relate his fears to his own mortality; he observes the others in the room without seeing his own participation.

The word *cigány* appears in the original text of "Slap," "Pioneer," and "Hospital"; I have translated it as "gypsy" rather than "Roma," because "Roma" sounds anachronistic and overly careful (and is rejected by many Hungarian *cigányok*). There is no ideal translation of *cigány*, but "gypsy" comes closer than "Roma" does.

I could explain more details but see no need to do so; the poems will come through on their own, and readers can discover details in their own way and time.

I am grateful to everyone who made this book possible: to Gyula Jenei and Marianna Fekete, who reviewed my translations over a period of two years and gave me numerous helpful comments; to *Literary Matters* and *The Massachusetts Review*, for publishing some of the translations; to Dr. Claudia MacMillan, Dr. Larry Allums, the Louise and Donald Cowan Center for Education, and the Dallas Institute of Humanities and Culture, for inviting us in the fall of 2019; and to Will Evans and Deep Vellum. This project came out of solitude, dialogue, and reception; may the book return to these three.

# Acknowledgments

The following six translations were initially published in journals:

"Standing Point" and "Chess": *Literary Matters*, Issue 11:3 (Spring/ Summer 2019).

"Piano," "Cemetery," and "Madeleine": *Literary Matters*, Issue 12:1 (Fall 2019).

"Scissors": *The Massachusetts Review*, Summer 2021.

Thank you all
for your support.
We do this for you,
and could not do
it without you.

DEEP
VELLUM

# PARTNERS

# pixel ||| texel

LIFE IN DEEP ELLUM

EMBREY FAMILY
FOUNDATION

COMMON DESK
COWORKING

**ALLRED**
CAPITAL MANAGEMENT
*of*
**RAYMOND JAMES**®

## ADDITIONAL DONORS, CONT'D

| | |
|---|---|
| Mark Haber | Scott & Katy Nimmons |
| Mary Cline | Sherry Perry |
| Maynard Thomson | Sydneyann Binion |
| Michael Reklis | Stephen Harding |
| Mike Soto | Stephen Williamson |
| Mokhtar Ramadan | Susan Carp |
| Nikki & Dennis Gibson | Susan Ernst |
| Patrick Kukucka | Theater Jones |
| Patrick Kutcher | Tim Perttula |
| Rev. Elizabeth & Neil Moseley | Tony Thomson |
| Richard Meyer | |

## SUBSCRIBERS

| | | |
|---|---|---|
| Margaret Terwey | Nicole Yurcaba | Jarratt Willis |
| Ben Fountain | Jennifer Owen | Heustis Whiteside |
| Gina Rios | Melanie Nicholls | Samuel Herrera |
| Elena Rush | Alan Glazer | Heidi McElrath |
| Courtney Sheedy | Michael Doss | Jeffrey Parker |
| Caroline West | Matt Bucher | Carolyn Surbaugh |
| Brian Bell | Katarzyna Bartoszynska | Stephen Fuller |
| Charles Dee Mitchell | Michael Binkley | Kari Mah |
| Cullen Schaar | Erin Kubatzky | Matt Ammon |
| Harvey Hix | Martin Piñol | Elif Ağanoğlu |
| Jeff Lierly | Michael Lighty | |
| Elizabeth Simpson | Joseph Rebella | |

# AVAILABLE NOW FROM DEEP VELLUM

SHANE ANDERSON · *After the Oracle* · USA

MICHÈLE AUDIN · *One Hundred Twenty-One Days* · translated by Christiana Hills · FRANCE

BAE SUAH · *Recitation* · translated by Deborah Smith · SOUTH KOREA

MARIO BELLATIN · *Mrs. Murakami's Garden* · translated by Heather Cleary · *Beauty Salon* · translated by Shook · MEXICO

EDUARDO BERTI · *The Imagined Land* · translated by Charlotte Coombe · ARGENTINA

CARMEN BOULLOSA · *Texas: The Great Theft* · *Before* · *Heavens on Earth* · translated by Samantha Schnee · Peter Bush · Shelby Vincent · MEXICO

MAGDA CARNECI · *FEM* · translated by Sean Cotter · ROMANIA

LEILA S. CHUDORI · *Home* · translated by John H. McGlynn · INDONESIA

MATHILDE CLARK · *Lone Star* · translated by Martin Aitken · DENMARK

SARAH CLEAVE, ed. · *Banthology: Stories from Banned Nations* · IRAN, IRAQ, LIBYA, SOMALIA, SUDAN, SYRIA & YEMEN

LOGEN CURE · *Welcome to Midland: Poems* · USA

ANANDA DEVI · *Eve Out of Her Ruins* · translated by Jeffrey Zuckerman · MAURITIUS

PETER DIMOCK · *Daybook from Sheep Meadow* · USA

CLAUDIA ULLOA DONOSO · *Little Bird*, translated by Lily Meyer · PERU/NORWAY

RADNA FABIAS · *Habitus* · translated by David Colmer · CURAÇAO/NETHERLANDS

ROSS FARRAR · *Ross Sings Cheree & the Animated Dark: Poems* · USA

ALISA GANIEVA · *Bride and Groom* · *The Mountain and the Wall* · translated by Carol Apollonio · RUSSIA

FERNANDA GARCIA LAU · *Out of the Cage* · translated by Will Vanderhyden · ARGENTINA

ANNE GARRÉTA · *Sphinx* · *Not One Day* · *In/concrete* · translated by Emma Ramadan · FRANCE

JÓN GNARR · *The Indian* · *The Pirate* · *The Outlaw* · translated by Lytton Smith · ICELAND

GOETHE · *The Golden Goblet: Selected Poems* · *Faust, Part One* · translated by Zsuzsanna Ozsváth and Frederick Turner · GERMANY

SARA GOUDARZI · *The Almond in the Apricot* · USA

NOEMI JAFFE · *What are the Blind Men Dreaming?* · translated by Julia Sanches & Ellen Elias-Bursac · BRAZIL

CLAUDIA SALAZAR JIMÉNEZ · *Blood of the Dawn* · translated by Elizabeth Bryer · PERU

PERGENTINO JOSÉ · *Red Ants* · MEXICO

TAISIA KITAISKAIA · *The Nightgown & Other Poems* · USA

SONG LIN · *The Gleaner Song: Selected Poems* · translated by Dong Li · CHINA

JUNG YOUNG MOON · *Seven Samurai Swept Away in a River* · *Vaseline Buddha* · translated by Yewon Jung · SOUTH KOREA

KIM YIDEUM · *Blood Sisters* · translated by Ji yoon Lee · SOUTH KOREA

JOSEFINE KLOUGART · *Of Darkness* · translated by Martin Aitken · DENMARK

YANICK LAHENS · *Moonbath* · translated by Emily Gogolak · HAITI

FOUAD LAROUI · *The Curious Case of Dassoukine's Trousers* · translated by Emma Ramadan · MOROCCO

# FORTHCOMING FROM DEEP VELLUM

MARIO BELLATIN • *Etchapare* • translated by Shook • MEXICO

CAYLIN CARPA-THOMAS • *Iguana Iguana* • USA

MIRCEA CĂRTĂRESCU • *Solenoid* • translated by Sean Cotter • ROMANIA

TIM COURSEY • *Driving Lessons* • USA

ANANDA DEVI • *When the Night Agrees to Speak to Me* • translated by Kazim Ali • MAURITIUS

DHUMKETU • *The Shehnai Virtuoso* • translated by Jenny Bhatt • INDIA

LEYLÂ ERBIL • *A Strange Woman* • translated by Nermin Menemencioğlu & Amy Marie Spangler • TURKEY

ALLA GORBUNOVA • *It's the End of the World, My Love* • translated by Elina Alter • RUSSIA

NIVEN GOVINDEN • *Diary of a Film* • GREAT BRITAIN

GYULA JENEI • *Always Different* • translated by Diana Senechal · HUNGARY

DIA JUBAILI • *No Windmills in Basra* • translated by Chip Rosetti • IRAQ

ELENI KEFALA • *Time Stitches* • translated by Peter Constantine • CYPRUS

UZMA ASLAM KHAN • *The Miraculous True History of Nomi Ali* • PAKISTAN

ANDREY KURKOV • *Grey Bees* • translated by Boris Dralyuk • UKRAINE

JORGE ENRIQUE LAGE • *Freeway La Movie* • translated by Lourdes Molina • CUBA

TEDI LÓPEZ MILLS • *The Book of Explanations* • translated by Robin Myers • MEXICO

ANTONIO MORESCO • *Clandestinity* • translated by Richard Dixon • ITALY

FISTON MWANZA MUJILA • *The Villain's Dance* • translated by Roland Glasser • DEMOCRATIC REPUBLIC OF CONGO

N. PRABHAKARAN • *Diary of a Malayali Madman* • translated by Jayasree Kalathil • INDIA

THOMAS ROSS • *Miss Abracadabra* • USA

IGNACIO RUIZ-PÉREZ • *Isles of Firm Ground* • translated by Mike Soto • MEXICO

LUDMILLA PETRUSHEVSKAYA • *Kidnapped: A Crime Story* • translated by Marian Schwartz • RUSSIA

NOAH SIMBLIST, ed. • *Tania Bruguera: The Francis Effect* • CUBA

S. YARBERRY • *A Boy in the City* • USA